THE COST
IN
PENTECOST

THE COST
IN
PENTECOST

by

Father Joseph E. Orsini, Ed. D.

Logos International
Plainfield, N.J.

Nihil Obstat:
The Most Reverend James L. Schad
Vicar General and Censor Deputatus

Imprimatur:
The Most Reverend George H. Guilfoyle
Bishop of Camden

I dedicate this book to my thirteen-year-old nephew, Dominick Orsini, whose life and death brought many to the Jesus for whom he lived and died.

Other books by Father Orsini:

Hear My Confession
Papa Bear's Favorite Italian Dishes

Contents

Introduction

The "cost" in Pentecost was and is the death of Jesus on the cross of Calvary. He paid the cost once and for all. As Christians, we are called not only to share in this victory and triumph, but as His body, to share in the cost. There are major areas of concern in our lives as Spirit-filled and Spirit-led Christians which are of themselves, invitations to delve deeeply into the mystery of suffering and to live out its practical applications.

The charismatic renewal had and has much to teach us concerning the victorious Christian life, but that is not the whole story. With this book, I invite the reader into traditionally non-charismatic areas and to discover the fullness of the Gospel message. The Gospel *is* the answer to all the questions and problems of our lives.

I believe in, and have had, firsthand experience with the charismatic dimension of the Christian life. I have seen miracles of healing and I have also seen those not healed. I have seen miracles of prophecy fulfilled gloriously and I have also seen and felt the ominous "silence of God." There are simple answers to the confusions of our vision but they are not simplistic.

The proof of the Christian life is to live out, sometimes painfully, what is implied in the cross. Great spiritual gifts are no guarantee that we are following the Way which Jesus says we must walk.

Jesus tells us in Matthew 7:21-23, "Not all who sound religious are really godly people. They may refer to me as 'Lord,' but still won't get to heaven. For the decisive question is whether they obey my Father in heaven. At the Judgment many will tell me, 'Lord, Lord, we told others about you and used your name to cast out demons and to do other great miracles.' But I will reply, 'you have never been mine. . . .' "

Jesus is the only answer, but the problem that remains is to *apply* that answer to the important questions. At the center of all the questions we can ask is: "What is it going to cost me to follow Jesus?"

Jesus answers in Luke 14:27-28 ". . . No one can be my disciple who does not carry his own cross and follow me. But don't begin until you count the cost."

This book attempts to count the cost and to say that it's all worth it.

It has not been easy to follow the Lord. The pathway has been strewn with sharp, cutting stones and obstacles. There have been times when the darkness was oppressive and overwhelming. What is the cross, after all, which Jesus says we must carry in order to be His disciple? It is dying to one's self. That is never easy.

Salvation is a free gift which cannot be earned or bought, but to participate in salvation brings us to the cross and nails us there. It hurts, but it liberates. That process of liberation involves our total lives. Pentecost gives us the power to be His witnesses by equipping us with the charismatic gifts and making to grow in us the indispensable fruits of the Holy Spirit.

The fruits of the Spirit are "love, joy, peace, patience, kindness, goodness, faithfulness, gentleness and self-control" (Gal. 5:22). The unseen work of the Spirit in the endeavor to make these fruits mature in the life of a Christian is to take the role of the dresser of the vineyard. The dresser *prunes* the vine, *cuts* away dead growth, sometimes saws back lives branches, to encourage what remains to produce fruit in abundance. Cutting, pruning, and sawing seem to be brutally painful, but they are necessary for vigorous production.

We are called to produce this fruit in our lives to provide nourishment for the whole body of Christ. The gifts, prophecy, healing, miracles, tongues and interpretation of tongues, special faith, words of wisdom and knowledge are also necessary and beautiful, but they are the foliage on the vine. It is good to recall the incident where Jesus cursed the foliage-covered fig tree because, although its large and lush leaves promised delectable and nourishing fruit, it didn't have any. The gifts without the fruits are attractive but really don't offer substantial food. We can't live on leaves, but leaves and fruit together—this gives us beauty and sustenance.

The most important condition we can offer to the Lord and His Spirit in this life-changing work, is yieldedness; that is about all we need, for the Lord does the rest. We must be ready to yield to His word, the direct leadings of His Spirit and the spiritual authority of His Church.

My purpose for writing this book is to attempt to clarify these and other important issues in our life in Christ. I pray the Lord will use this book as an instrument for every Christian who reads it to be led to Him and be transformed by the power of the Holy Spirit into a more perfect reflector of the Light in a world covered by darkness. The time has come to stop talking about Christianity and start acting in such a way that our love will draw others to Jesus.

THE COST
IN
PENTECOST

PART I

JESUS AND YOU

1

Are You Hot or Cold?

I know your works: you are neither cold nor hot. Would that you were cold or hot! So, because you are lukewarm, and neither cold nor hot, I will spew you out of my mouth. For you say, I am rich, I have prospered, and I need nothing; not knowing that you are wretched, pitiable, poor, blind, and naked. Therefore I counsel you to buy from me gold refined by fire, that you may be rich, and white garments to clothe you and to keep the shame of your nakedness from being seen, and salve to anoint your eyes, that you may see. Those whom I love, I reprove and chasten; so be zealous and repent. Behold, I stand at the door and knock; if any one hears my voice and opens the door, I will come in to him and eat with him, and he with me (Rev. 3:15-20 RSV)

There is a story told about a village church that was discovered to be on fire by parishioners who were coming to morning service. They called the volunteer fire department which arrived in a few minutes but did not have enough hose to reach the church from the nearest fire hydrant. Buckets were quickly gotten and parishioners lined up to pass those buckets to the firemen.

Someone watching the others do their work said to one of the volunteer firemen, "Man, this is the first time I have ever seen you at church." The fireman replied, "It's the first time I've ever seen this church on fire." Someone else looking at all those church members passing the buckets to the firemen remarked, "It's also the first time the members of this church ever did anything together."

What is the temperature in your church? What is your own temperature? Are you hot or cold? Or, maybe, somewhere "in between" with no temperature at all: neither hot nor cold. In other words, just right! It's not just right that way. The Lord says, "It's just blah!"

In the Book of Revelation the Lord speaks to the church in Laodicea. "I know your works: you are neither cold nor hot. Would that you were cold or hot! So, because you are lukewarm, and neither cold nor hot, I will spew you out of my mouth."

There may be some sense in not going way off to the left or way off to the right, but trying instead to keep a middle course. Still, there are those on the left and on the right who will insist that standing for something is better than standing for nothing or not knowing where you stand at all. People who don't take any stand at all usually get pushed in all directions. Standing for nothing, they don't know in which direction to go when the going gets rough, so they have a tendency to fly off in all directions at the same time.

The church at Laodicea thought it stood for the Lord. They thought they knew where they stood, but temperature was a problem with the people of that church. They could never get excited about anything. The thermometer never read hot or cold, and the Lord said: "I will spew you out of my mouth."

When I was a kid we used to refer to something or someone great as "hot stuff." Today kids say the same thing with this phrase: "Man, that's cool." They mean it's good. No one who was lukewarm has ever been called great. A lukewarm person is neither hot nor cold, just lukewarm, like coffee that has been sitting too long. Jesus didn't have much time for those stale coffee people or churches. "Because you are lukewarm . . . I will spew you out of my mouth."

Jesus died on the cross for the sins of people who blew too hot or too cold in their lifetime. He also died for the lukewarm ones, the fence-sitters, the ones who never take a stand on anything. They didn't participate in the near-riot that attended His crucifixion, and they didn't defend Him either. They just stood aside. He died for those people, too.

Now that Jesus has risen from the dead in glory, He won't tolerate lukewarmness any longer. He forgives the hot and He forgives the cold, as they repent of their sins and turn to Him for forgiveness. The lukewarm, because of their very nature, don't think they need any forgiveness. They never did anything right, and they never did anything wrong. "I know you," says Jesus. "You are neither hot nor cold . . . you are lukewarm . . . and . . . I will spew you out of my mouth."

Jesus is alive. He rose from the dead. He is in control. The living Lord must have a living church. He doesn't want people to die. He wants them to live. That is what His forgiveness is all about. He gives life, vibrant, pulsating, surging life. Life in Christ, with a living faith in Him and a living love that comes from Him, leaves no room at all for lukewarmness. That kind of stuff, says Jesus, makes me sick.

I know your works, Jesus says. He is alive and He is God. He knows all of us. It isn't a very comforting thought for people who are trying to get along on their own, as so many are, not exactly challenging God but not loyal to Him either. It is very uncomfortable to find out, under those circumstances, that God knows exactly who and what you are.

Jesus has His eyes on us. He is Lord and He knows it. If we know that He is Lord, then we had better live as if we did. Jesus did not die for nothing. He exercises His lordship in a most gracious way. He invites us to come, to find forgiveness in Him, to find life in Him, to go all the way with Him, all the way.

We can turn away, but He is still Lord. We can pick our way down the path of life, avoiding open commitment to Him and open rejection of Him. We can do that if we choose. But He has something to say to us: ". . . Because you are lukewarm, I will vomit you out of my mouth."

It is a clear fact that the despised and rejected of Jesus' time were more easily drawn to Him than the respectable people who were convinced that they could do very well without Him. How often this appears in the Gospels: the publicans and sinners drew near to hear Him. Without Him they didn't stand a chance. The fine respectable people stood on the sidelines and criticized Him. They were religious people, but they had no use for Him. Going with Him would mean they would have to admit they were sinners like everyone else, and needed forgiveness as much as anyone else. That was a little too much for them to take, and it's still a little too much to take for many of us, especially if we are respectable Christians who don't want to appear fanatical.

There is one thing we can be sure of and that is Jesus. It makes me feel good to see young and old people get excited about Jesus in the charismatic renewal. Sometimes their enthusiasm about Jesus does not always take acceptable forms, and observers who practice a sensible and orderly form of Christianity are turned off. Whenever someone young or old commits himself to Jesus altogether, no matter how he does it, it makes me feel good all over. I can understand how the Lord feels about lukewarmness—it makes Him sick to the stomach. It should make us sick too.

Most of the people I have met in the charismatic renewal, who are following Jesus all the way, have strong convictions. They know Jesus died for them personally. They know Jesus forgives and they experience His forgiveness. They know their lives have changed through Jesus' ministry of the baptism with the Holy Spirit. They know what the end of all this is going to be; a glorious resurrection from the dead like the Resurrection of Jesus himself. They try to love where otherwise they would hate, or just be indifferent. They can't stand by and see someone else hurt without going to help them. Conviction works, right here and now.

There is no lukewarmness in that conviction. Some of them may be carried away in some of their convictions, but they are not lukewarm. Jesus describes how lukewarm people react: they say, "I am rich, I have prospered, and I need nothing." "Not so," says Jesus. "You don't know how wretched, poor, pitiable, blind and naked you really are." Older Christians, who imagine it is their prerogative to criticize those who are totally involved in this new and suspicious form of fanaticism found in the charismatic renewal, don't know how wretched, pitiable, poor, naked, and blind they are. On the other hand, some over enthusiastic Christians made new through the charismatic renewal seem to think they are the only ones who have the true way and look down on their brothers and sisters in Christ who haven't found it yet. They are just as wretched, pitiable, poor, naked and blind.

"Therefore," says the living Lord to all of us, because He wants all of us to come alive and *stay* alive, "I counsel you to buy from me gold refined by fire, that you may be rich, and white garments to clothe you and to keep the shame of your nakedness from being seen, and salve to anoint your eyes, that you may see. Those whom I love, I reprove and chasten; so be zealous and repent. Behold I stand at the door and knock; if any one hears my voice and opens the door, I will come in to him and eat with him, and he with me."

In an old hymn, the followers of Jesus were cautioned against thinking that they could go to heaven on flowery beds of ease. Today some of us think we are going to get to heaven on the fine, fat cushions of our church pews. Faith is a personal thing between us and God. Either we have it or we don't. If we don't, it doesn't make any difference how many times we plunk ourselves down on the cushion of that pew.

The same thing goes for all those pious people who as the result of their salvation or charismatic experiences now consider themselves religious and never, or hardly ever, set foot in a church.

They don't want to commit themselves. Nobody is going to get by who picks and chooses among the teachings of Jesus and holds only those that are convenient or pleasing. Christ knows us and our works. It would be better for us to be openly hostile to Him than to think we can do it *our* way. It is His way or none at all.

Jesus does not call us to a life of ease. Those whom I love, He says, I reprove and chasten. Commit yourself to me, says Jesus, in repentance and faith. "I am the way, the truth, and the life" (John 14:6).

2

Where the Action Isn't!

But be ye doers of the word, and not hearers only deceiving your own selves. (James 1:22 KJV)

There are a lot of "gaps" around today. One that comes immediately to mind is the "generation gap" that exists between young people and their elders, between those whose experience reaches back through World War II to times of want and depression and those who, until recently, have by and large experienced only relatively affluent times.

Then there is the "credibility gap," that large space between what we are often told and the way things really are. Today many people suspect the news is not news any more, but some kind of fancy product manufactured by newsmaking agencies. There are many "gaps" between truth and fiction, between what people think they are and what they really are. Each one of these would be worth discussing, but I want to zero in on one I have coined, the "action gap."

It sticks out in the world, it raises its ugly head in the churches, and it spoils life for people everywhere. The action gap was what St. James was thinking about when he said: " . . . Be ye doers of the word, and not hearers only, deceiving your own selves."

The action gap, as St. James saw it in people of his time, and as we can see it in people of our time—indeed, as we can see it in ourselves—is a big gaping hole which exists between what we say and what we actually do, what we preach and what we practice.

You can find the action gap almost everywhere these days. Take pollution, for example. People talk about it all the time. They are all complaining about what is happening to our air, water, and soil, not to mention the destructive results of these vital elements of life for our health. Studies on the problem are appearing all over the place. Government feels it has to do something about the increasing anti-pollution sentiments of its constituents. Laws are passed and standards are established. But where is the action? In many instances action is just put off, in the hope evidently that the problem somehow will disappear.

Take law and order as another example. Most people are for law and order. They want strong laws to protect their lives and property, their rights, their own best interests, and they want these laws vigorously enforced. But they are not nearly as interested in seeing that others get the same consideration. We may be the most vigorous advocates of law and order, yet we violate the most obvious laws in the most casual way. We deliberately go through stop signs, throw trash onto the sides of the highways, and blatantly disregard the rights of our neighbors. Our casual gossip openly slanders the good names of others, evidently on the theory that nobody will notice and nobody will care. This is an action gap.

Well-intentioned efforts to help the poorer peoples of the world have often resulted in lining the pockets of people who couldn't even pretend to be poor. The poor are still hungry, and the well-fed are just putting on weight. That is an action gap.

Of course we can say that this is somebody else's problem. "I am not involved, I don't have any responsibility for it." If someone says that in a society where people have the right to express themselves freely, the right to vote, the responsibility to govern themselves, then you have another action gap.

It is still true, as it always was, "what you *are* speaks so loud that I cannot hear what you *say*." The action gap can come home to each one of us with a thunderclap.

The Epistle of James speaks plainly and is full of sayings that people can remember: ". . . Faith by itself, if it has no works, is dead" (2:17 RSV). ". . . The anger of man does not work the righteousness of God" (1:20 RSV). "You desire and do not have; so you kill" (4:2 rsv). ". . . Judgment is without mercy to one who has shown no mercy" (2:13 RSV). ". . . Be ye doers of the word, and not hearers only, deceiving your own selves" (1:22 KJV). James talks to *all* of us. If we refuse to act on our convictions, when we know what the will of God is for all of us, we are deceiving, not God, but only ourselves. James does not mince words.

James knew Jesus. He called himself a slave of God and of the Lord Jesus Christ. He was a man of faith, believing Jesus Christ, putting his whole confidence in Jesus, entrusting his life to Jesus. A man like that, said James, can't be indecisive and inactive. He has to take a stand, and his faith must be an active, working faith.

The death of the Lord, His Resurrection, and the coming of the Spirit at Pentecost changed James, the apostles, and the disciples. Changed men and women were the result *then* of God's saving acts and it is the same thing that happens to men and women today when they know Jesus, accept His forgiving love, follow Him, give their lives to Him, and are baptized by Him with the Holy Spirit.

James knew Jesus. That makes him quite a man. We have to admire his plain, blunt and simple way of saying things because that must have been the way he did things too. He said, "If any one thinks he is religious, and does not bridle his tongue but rather deceives his heart, this man's religion is vain" (1:26). "My brethren, show no partiality as you hold the faith 'of our Lord Jesus Christ, the Lord of glory" (2:1). That admonition applies to all of us Christians, liberal and conservative, charismatic and

11

non-charismatic, evangelical and episcopal, Catholic and Protestant.

This is the one place in the whole New Testament that I know where Jesus is referred to as the Lord of glory. God is always called a God of glory, and James identifies Jesus with the God of glory. This is the way to do it, he said: "Be doers of the Word of God and not just hearers. If you fail to do, neglect to do, refuse to do, you delude yourselves."

There is a good deal of delusion around these days among the ranks of both charismatic and non-charismatic Christianity. I have seen both men and women using their salvation, their Pentecostal experiences as wedges between themselves and their spouses, families, and friends to claim some kind of importance or spiritual superiority. There are too many of us who preach brotherhood and fellowship among denominations but who secretly hold our own theologies as really superior and closer to the truth.

I remember two distinct occasions separated by a five-year span, and both involving the same gentleman, in which I encountered this kind of prejudice.

I had twice been invited to address the same interdenominational gathering with my testimony, once in 1971 and again in 1976. Both times a dour-looking man approached me and began to berate me soundly for still belonging to the Roman Catholic church. An ex-Catholic by his own admission, he called the Catholic church "that great whore of Babylon." "You only think you're saved," he told me angrily. "But you can't be saved and filled with the Spirit if you still belong to *that* church!"

I wept. My heart ached because this man who called me "brother" had missed the joy of Christ.

As Christians we complain about the abuses of politicians, the ravages of poverty, social and racial injustice, hatred and crime, and that's all we do. But we refuse to get involved in doing, in practical and concrete action that costs us something personally. That is why the non-Christian and non-believing world doesn't take what we say seriously. It sees too clearly that we are sayers and not doers.

What causes an action gap? What keeps us from putting into practice what we preach? We preach that Jesus died for all men everywhere. Then we act as if He died just for our own little select group. "Faith by itself," said James, "if it has no works, is dead."

Sometimes we are afraid to act because we don't know what other people will say. Of whom are we afraid, anyway, when the Father forgives our sins for the sake of Jesus? When the Holy Spirit calls us to follow Him, the Lord of glory? The greatest condemnation Jesus made of the *religious* people who were always criticizing Him is that they had more regard for the opinions of men than they had for the opinion of God.

We have been given the greatest example of how our Christian lives should be lived in Jesus. St. Peter says of Him: "It was to this that God called you; because Christ himself suffered for you and left you an example, so that you would follow in his steps. He committed no sin; no one ever heard a lie come from his lips. When he was insulted he did not answer back with an insult; when he suffered he did not threaten, but placed his hopes in God, the righteous Judge. Christ himself carried our sins in his body to the cross, so that we might die to sin and live for righteousness. By his wounds you have been healed" (1 Pet. 2:21-24 TEV).

Let the healing wave go forth! It has to be carried by people like you and me. There are no others. "For the time is come that judgment must begin at the house of God . . . what shall the end be of them that obey not the gospel of God? (1 Pet. 4:17 KJV). *"Be a doer of the word."* If you suffer for it, well and good. Those who suffer by following the will of God can be assured that their spirits belong to a faithful God. Commit your spirits to Him, said Peter, doing what is right and good.

This is the word of God. Not mine, His. The only way to bridge the action gap is to go ahead and *do* the word and will of God.

It is possible to repent of past actions which have dishonored God. It is not only possible, it is necessary. Repentance is the first step on the bridge to action. We can repent of the fact that we have only been hearers and not doers of the word and resolve to *really* follow Jesus in the future. Fathers who claim authority over their families, but recognize no responsibility of love toward them, have repented and gone on to better things by following Jesus in word and action. People who have made a mess of their lives have repented and found a new life in following Jesus in word and action. The renewal of life comes from the Father by faith in Jesus. "By his own will," says James, "he brought us into being through the word of truth, so that we should have first place among all his creatures." (1:18 TEV)

Let there be no mistake about this: the word of truth is Jesus. It was that for James, and it has to be that for us. He is the truth. He is also the way and the life. It is all in Him. By Him there is access, a new way, to the Father. By faith in Him, salvation comes with *new* attitudes, *new* resolves, *new* determination, and *new* action. He died for all, that they who live by Him in faith might not live to themselves but rather to Him who for their sakes died and rose again.

That's it. It is the word of God. Hear it, believe it, do it! Anything else is self-deception, self-delusion, and eventually self-destruction. We must close that action gap in our lives, the gap between guilt and forgiveness. We must take Jesus and go with Him. Everyone who looks deeply into the gospel of Jesus that sets men free, and stays with it, who is not just a forgetful hearer but a doer of the word, not simply a listener but one who puts his faith into practice, that one will be blessed by God in His doing.

3

Questions, Always Questions!

And it is for this reason that I suffer these things. But I am still full of confidence, because I know whom I have trusted, and I am sure that he is able to keep safe until that Day what he has entrusted to me. (2 Tim. 1:12 TEV)

When children begin to ask "Why?" it's a sign they are beginning to grow up and to think for themselves. Nevertheless it's still a little upsetting to have them ask their questions when we don't have answers or if we can't give them answers in language they understand.

God has similar problems with us. We are always asking "Why?" There is nothing really wrong with asking the questions; it shows that we are human and that we are thinking. Why do things happen as they do? Why must disappointment be a part of life? Why sickness, suffering, despair, and finally death? Why? Why now? Why not later on? Why this person? Or (more frequently) why me?

Obviously there are some things about the eternal plans of God that are hard to explain in the language we all know and use, the language of time. We always think in terms of length, width, height, and time, the four dimensions in which we live and move and have our being. We find it impossible to even think of ourselves in the framework of eternity where there is no time, and so we are always asking questions about eternity and the timeless plans of the eternal God.

God knows what He is doing and why He is doing it. But the problem is much like the one we face with our children; how are we going to understand? That must be why God sent His Son into the world, not to answer all of our questions, not to remove all the mysteries of life and of death, but to give us all someone in whom we can believe, someone we can follow, someone to go the way we have to go, someone to offer forgiveness for the past and hope for the future, someone to open the door to heaven for us. That someone is Jesus, our Brother and God's Son.

St. Paul had plenty of reason to ask "Why?" He had suffered much, not through his own fault, as many of us do, but because he was a man of God in a world of evil men. He could still ask "why?" and wonder about it, but he had Jesus to trust and follow. "He saved us," Paul said, "and called us to be his own people, not because of what we have done, but because of his own purpose and grace. He gave us this grace by means of Christ Jesus before the beginning of time, but now it has been revealed to us through the coming of our Savior, Christ Jesus. He has ended the power of death, and through the Good News has revealed immortal life. God has appointed me to proclaim the Good News as an apostle and teacher, and it is for this reason that I suffer these things. But I am still full of confidence, because I know whom I have trusted, and I am sure that he is able to keep safe until that Day what he has entrusted to me" (2 Tim. 1:9-12 TEV).

Not long ago, an entertainer and a political radical said, "I am interested in anything about revolt, disorder, chaos, especially activity that has no meaning. That seems to me to be the road to freedom." A famous English artist said, "Life itself is a tragic thing. We watch ourselves from the cradle, performing into decay. Man now realizes that he has to play out the game without a reason."

16

These are statements of thinking people. In words and actions that amount to self-destruction, men are crying out in their bewilderment, sick of living because they can find no meaning in it all, no sense, no purpose, no answer to "Why?" Our technology has opened up new areas of knowledge. There is more untapped power than man can possibly use. Still no worthwhile answers are emerging from the natural sciences to our ultimate questions.

The typical college graduate today is bright, intelligent, and agnostic. He is almost proud of the fact that he can't know anything for certain but that does not stop him from interpreting life. He sees how insignificant individual people are on this crowded and tiny planet. He senses the great sweeps of time that pass while man is born, lives, and dies. He tries to find some vague hope in the upward movement of what is called evolution. In his heart of hearts, however, he has trouble believing that the modern world shows really important basic improvement over the past. He is sensitive to the pain and suffering of the world around him. The tough and the ruthless so often seem to prosper, the good and innocent seem to suffer. He is very aware of the God that some people are always talking about. The God who holds all the cards, both judge and jury, making demands and then punishing people who are unable to carry them out. To him God looks like the creation of some man's mind, with no regard for human life, unmoved by the slaughter that takes place in the world, somewhat primitive, like the people who concocted Him.

Looking at life itself, the modern, thinking man often has great difficulty in finding any purpose in it all. Everything seems to be the result of a blind accident. There seems to be no explanation, no reason, no significant relationship to an ultimate order. It is the kind of thinking that has been drilled into us. "Don't believe in anything that can't be proved!" All proof is empirical, something you can see. All modern philosophy is committed to that idea. Still there are some who are optimistic because they hope that somehow, by education, by scientific inquiry into the structures of

17

life, they will be able to discover some meaning in it all. Others take the approach that there is no use because all existence is under the heavy hand of a blind fate and no amount of intelligence, good will, hard work, or thrift is going to change anything. Therefore, live for today, tomorrow we'll all be dead.

If a man doesn't have any hope in God, then pessimism is a lot more justified than optimism. We have a good deal less reason to hope today that diplomacy or war or industrial production or scientific advances or philosophy of any kind is going to make this world a better place than it was before.

In a completely secular world like ours where people lived as St. Paul said, "without God and without hope in the world," he had the guts to say: "I am still full of confidence, for I know whom I have trusted."

The most daring thing anyone can say is "I know." There is no hesitancy, no qualification, in that statement. It is not "I think" or "I hope" or "I imagine," it is "I know." The claim is staggering in any age and today can be interpreted as very bold or very stupid. St. Paul did not claim to have knowledge about something or someone. It is knowledge *of* that he talks about. He knows someone, really knows Him. That is the way faith talks when it knows what it's talking about. Paul was talking about Jesus. He knew that God matters, not just that God exists, but He matters. There are a lot of people who are ready to admit that God exists, but that is not enough. There must be an acknowledgment that we are attached to Him.

Some men have cut the string that ties them to a personal God, the God who created and sustains the world. When modern man began to feel that God had become an unnecessary assumption for scientific life in the twentieth century, he cut the string that attached him to the center of reality. Men who decide that God does not matter, that they can manage very well without Him, manage only to bring about their own collapse. The truth is that when we try to do without God, we collapse. We cut the thread that holds us in living touch with the living God.

God matters! He matters just as much as air for our lungs. As a priest, I have been called to the bedsides of more dying people than I would like to remember. It is always the same; always they struggle and gasp frantically for air. In the same way, anyone who is sensitive can "hear" the choking of men in our age. Suffocating with fear and bewilderment, hurrying towards they know not what, without purpose or direction; all because they are trying to do it without God.

Why do men have such trouble believing in God? Some of them say they cannot believe because they cannot know who God is. So they refuse to affirm *that* He is. Many have even given up the search for God and have stopped asking questions altogether.

St. Paul in Acts 17 describes the movement toward God as a "groping." He is, said Paul, not far from us. Too many people today claim the search for God is too tough or too perilous, so they quit and conclude "there is no God." Claiming to be scientific, they are all too ready to judge by appearances. Actually, appearances can be very deceptive. It may appear that there is no God or if there is, He must be on vacation. But the conclusion that there is no God is a radical decision for which there can be no rational justification. A man can try to think his way into a world where God is no longer necessary, but in his deeper inner being he senses that he is probably wrong.

A lot of things can be explained today by science that were mysteries years ago. Scientific explanations have increased and supposedly, the need for God has decreased. That, too, has no rational justification. God does not exist to provide explanations, but to fill a need, a deep human need inside all of us. St. Paul had that need, so have I, and so have you. "I know," Paul said, "whom I have believed." It is not merely a matter of intelligence or of understanding. This is an affair of the heart and spirit of man. St. Paul knew. It made a different man of him. He put all of his intelligence and all of his emotions into that one statement, "I know!'' And in that knowledge he became fully a man. It is not simply knowledge, but acknowledgment, recognition and commitment. It is commitment of everything a man is. It is what the Bible calls faith and it is the heart of the whole matter.

The church has always proclaimed that God became one of us so that we might directly experience Him, believe, and have life. ''He gave us this grace by means of Christ Jesus before the beginning of time,'' Paul said, ''but now it has been revealed to us through the coming of our Savior, Christ Jesus. He has ended the power of death and through the Good News has revealed immortal life'' (2 Tim. 1:9-10 TEV).

Now everything is different. It must be. It is different personally, for each of us. A man named Jesus lived and died, about that there can be no question. People of faith have consistently interpreted this fact along these lines: ''In Christ, God was reconciling the world to himself not counting our sins against us . . . He has committed to us a world of reconciliation . . . with faith in Christ I can do anything . . . for me living is Christ . . . I am full of confidence, I know Him, trust Him, and follow Him. I am sure He is able to keep safe until that great day of His whatever He has entrusted to me.''

Living by faith in Christ does not mean that we have the answers to all our questions. We can still ask ''Why?'' and some of our questions will probably never be answered to our satisfaction while we live. But we know that it's all right because He lives. He has risen from the dead and is our living Savior. We can have confidence in Him, and go forward to make the decisions that we have to make, using the intelligence He gave us.

St. Paul disclosed in what he wrote that there were a lot of decisions he had to make himself. Sometimes he wondered whether he had done the right thing. But he always knew Jesus. ''I know,'' he said, and he became a vital part of that young community all the members of which knew God in Jesus. They knew Him as Father. They knew Him in a new and vital fashion because of the coming of Jesus and His sending of the Holy Spirit. They knew something of the character of God. He saves. He can be depended upon. He gives hope for the future. He keeps safe until His own day everything He has entrusted to those who trust Him.

It is a living, vital thing to know Jesus and be close to Him, not to just feel close to Him, or think ourselves close to Him, but to *be* close to Him. It makes the difference between confident and cowardly living. In Jesus there is the dynamic presence of the Holy Spirit who empowers all of life. It is a real experience to know Him. It is real because it is totally human. It is great because the questions we are always asking fall into perspective and we are able to say "I don't know all the answers, but I know whom I have trusted, and of Him I am sure."

4

The Problem Is Us!

And I tell you more: whenever two of you on earth agree about anything you pray for, it will be done for you by my Father in heaven. For where two or three come together in my name, I am there with them. (Matt. 18:19-20 TEV)

Our world is like Humpty Dumpty—it is falling apart and nobody knows how to put it together again. The isolation and insulation we have from one another has become a hard fact of life. No one is spared this agony, whether rich or ghetto dweller, suburbanite or city dweller. Our modern world has made tremendous progress at the expense of significant relationships between people. When life was simpler, people knew each other, felt for each other and helped each other, not looking for anything in return. But in an age of mass production, mass advertising, and mass communication, we haven't the time nor the interest in one another. We have world alliances, world banks, world trade organizations, international diplomacy and feel the pressure that we had better make it all work, or else. We are in the midst of a great economic crisis and are told that economic disaster is just around the corner. That is just one crisis; others are on the way. No matter our social status or occupation, we are *all* part of the tension and nervous expectation in this stacked up, piled up world of ours. Breakdown of the economic, social, political and organized religious processes under which most of us live in this world could result in the greatest catastrophe that man has ever seen. No one in *this* world will be able to put it together again.

We have a message. A message from God to a sick, exploding, and fragmented humanity, living out its life in the last part of this twentieth century. Part of that message is found in these words of Jesus: "I tell you more, whenever two of you on earth agree about anything you pray for, it will be done for you by my Father in heaven. For where two or three come together in my name, I am there with them."

In Jesus we see a confidence in God the Father that is almost beyond belief. He never questions God; He takes Him at His word, and is always sure of Him. Sure of His Father, Jesus was always sure of himself. Of course as a man He had His moments; He felt the pressures of life deeply, as any man does. But fear, which is faith in failure, never conquered His heart. He knew God as a Father who wouldn't let His children down. He was obedient to His Father and in that obedience is our salvation. This man, this Jesus, a real man like us, was the chosen one of God, the anointed one, the Messiah, the Savior of the world. We can depend on Him, because He is Lord and He loves us. He died and rose again from the dead—for us. *He lives* and forgives. In Him there is life for anyone who responds in faith, who puts his confidence in Him. This message cuts through the whole morass of conflicting interests, currents and movements that promise so much and deliver so little to the churches and the world.

"Where two or three are gathered in my name, I am there with them." That is Jesus talking to us, all of us, the great and the small, whether bishops, government officials, families, groups, institutions, organizations, churches, or forgotten and lonely individuals. He is talking to all of us on whom the realization is dawning that the madness in the world is directly related to the way we have set our course to "go it alone," for the sake of ourselves alone, for the purposes of serving ourselves alone. This Jesus, Son of God, King of kings, who governs the whole universe, promises to be with us. It is His promise, as only He could make it. He promises this frightened, polarized and disoriented world of men that He will be here in it, among us, to heal, to guide and to enrich the lives of us who come together in His name, even if it's only two or three of us.

In Jesus, God comes closer and closer to us. But there are some who say: "So what? There have been other great men, but they are all gone now. Jesus is a 'has been' like the rest of them. He is nowhere close to me, He's gone and God is far away as He has always seemed to be. What can Jesus do for us today?" To this kind of doubt, hesitancy, and skepticism, Jesus speaks: "Where two or three come together in my name, I am there with you." He says it, He means it, and it is so.

This astounding and provable truth can be experienced and is capable of generating a revolution within the world of human relationships today. It is the truth that God in Jesus lives in this world of ours and that He truly forgives, in Jesus. God shows us His Father's heart and love in Jesus.

The breakdowns of our society—the class alienations and racial clashes, the horrendous divorce rates, the economic favoritism, the battered children, the drug and alcohol addiction, the broken families and decaying cities—these are just some of our problems. But really, *we* are the problem. As individuals and as groups, we just can't seem to get along. We are full of insecurities and guilt. Deep down inside, we feel we don't rate either with God or with anyone else. Because we feel inadequate, despite our pretensions, we become defensive. We rise up to defend our own little areas, our own little interests, our own race, our own nationalities, our own opinions and petty philosophies. We have very little faith and a lot of fear. Because we feel inadequate we focus our efforts and attention on ourselves, our own affairs, our own objectives—all in a vain and empty attempt to gain a level of superiority. That leaves little time for effective and constructive relationships with others.

In fact, we are not at all interested in others. In this kind of atmosphere there are very few of us who can tolerate the egotism and one-sidedness of demands of others, whether in our families, communities, churches, or groups. And a family or society in which every man is "out for himself" becomes a sinking ship. We struggle and go under even deeper. Unable to reach or understand one another, we only contribute to the longstanding, insoluble weaknesses and sicknesses that bring about death. There is no healing because there is no help.

How can God help in this situation? He has promised that whenever two or three gather together in the name of His Son, in the Spirit of Jesus, reconciling, redeeming, healing, and empowering will come also. Through Jesus, the Father calls us into fellowship with each other and with himself. He takes our fractured, lonely lives and fills us with love, peace, joy, and satisfaction. Jesus knows all about alienation and loneliness. He took that for us, and it is done with. Now He calls us individually, to espouse His name. The selfishness that allows us to disregard others in favor of ourselves is *the* root of all our trouble and stands between ourselves, others and God. Jesus' death pays for our selfishness and invites us to put it off so that we might be free to serve others.

There are whole communities of people throughout the world who have accepted this gracious act of God. They are found in the charismatic renewal, free associations of born-again evangelicals, and the traditional churches; but by whatever name they designate themselves, they gather together in Jesus' name to practice the skills of loving one another, caring for others, and carrying out Jesus' mission to the world. As He has promised, He is with them, and His presence is confirmed not only by signs and wonders, but by that peace which surpasses all understanding. These are ordinary people like you and me. Once they fended for themselves but at their invitation God has moved into their lives in Jesus. Jesus Christ is in them, and wherever they gather in His name He leads them into purposeful and effective action for the sake of the world in which we live. That is why they are called "Christians."

Christians, or followers of Jesus, are on the road to overcoming any former sense of frustration and inadequacy. When we know Jesus, there is no longer any struggle to rate, to count, to measure up in the eyes of men. God has graciously come to terms with us and in Jesus we are able to come to terms graciously with ourselves and one another. Incessant efforts to prove ourselves evaporates with the conviction that God accepts us *as we are*, accepts us as His own, cherishes us for the right things we do now, rather than for what we think we ought to have done. God forgives us because He loves us. He fills us with His Holy Spirit and manifests His presence in us by astounding spiritual gifts. Then we move with the uniting and inspiring knowledge that where two or three are gathered in Jesus' name, there, in our gathering, Jesus himself will be with us.

World conditions are different from what they were when the gospel message was first proclaimed, but the message still comes through loud and clear, developed technologies, new social systems, and international relations notwithstanding. God is in Jesus reconciling the world to himself. Not counting our sins against us, He has given us this word of reconciliation. It is His word for us, that, in the name of His Son, trusting His promise, we, such as we are, might live with courage, hope and determination, always showing love, which is the one thing our world needs more than anything else.

God's ruling principle found in the gospel is not manipulation, domination, or exploitation. It is not the sharp division of classes, clergy from laity, governors from the governed. It is not the apathy of some people to the needs of others. The ruling principle of God is the love of Jesus, and His reach for the world. Here the governing impulse, the mission, is to call all lost, wandering, and alienated men to the fellowship of God's people, to the inner peace and outer action which combine to give new life to people, and through them, touch the lives of others with that same new life.

5

Where Do We Belong?

And the Lord said, "What have you done? The voice of your brother's blood is crying to me from the ground. And now you are cursed from the ground, which has opened its mouth to receive your brother's blood from your hand. When you till the ground, it shall no longer yield to you its strength; you shall be a fugitive and a wanderer on the earth." Cain said to the Lord, "My punishment is greater than I can bear. Behold, thou hast driven me this day away from the ground; and from thy face I shall be hidden; and I shall be a fugitive and wanderer on the earth, and whoever finds me will slay me. (Gen. 4:10-14 RSV)

It is a hard thing to live without knowing where we belong, without having a place we can call home. Millions of people have found themselves in such circumstances. Refugee camps are not pleasant sights, filled as they are with people asking incessantly: "Where do we belong? Where is our place?"

Our world is filled today with spiritual refugees, wanderers, people without a proper place, wondering who they are and where they are going, unsatisfied with their lot, feeling unwanted, people without a home. Some have acquired a lot of things, yet they have nothing. They long for home, but cannot find it. Paradise is their dream, but that dream never seems to become a reality.

At the dawn of human history an envious man killed his brother in a fit of anger. God banished him from his place. The man said, "My punishment is heavier than I can bear; you have driven me away today from the ground, I must hide myself from your presence. I shall be a wanderer on earth, and anyone who meets me can kill me." The man had no place, and he was afraid.

Cain had a brother named Abel. Both recognized God, as any man in his right mind does. But one had faith and served God, while the other did not. One found he needed God to live happily, and the other did not. Abel, the man of faith, offered his sacrifice to God and it was accepted. Cain offered his sacrifice and it was not accepted. In anger born of jealousy Cain killed his brother and became a homeless wanderer.

Ever since then, this has been the story of mankind. This is the way many people deal with one another. They hurt, they harm, they kill. We all do it, those of us who think of ourselves as very religious and those of us who have no religion at all. With a word, with a gesture, we kill just as much as if we had taken an axe to another's neck. St. John said, "Any one who hates his brother is a murderer, and you know that no murderer has eternal life abiding in him" (1 John 3:15 RSV).

Eternal life is man's place—where he belongs—in God's plan. It is the place we have lost, all of us. We can't blame God. We lost it. "For all have sinned, and come short of the glory of God" (Rom. 3:23 KJV). The mark of Cain is upon us. We have done what we ought not to have done, and we have failed to do what we should have done. We are unfair. We are given to self-righteousness and pride, we think only of ourselves, and we do violence to one another. The mark of Cain is upon us, and we are restless. We wander from place to place, relationship to relationship. We feel sorry for ourselves, and we are afraid.

Not too long ago, some theologians made the headlines by

telling us that the modern city holds all the promise of paradise regained. It just isn't so. Even the theologians who seem always to be going after the latest fad in thinking have abandoned the idea they had so carefully fostered. The modern city is just another symptom of what is wrong with our world. Its streets are the scenes of violence which threaten to destroy any possibility of an orderly society. The modern city, with all of its imposing structures and marvelous conveniences is the most convincing evidence of all that humanity cannot find its way by its own efforts. Far from being a heaven on earth, the city is rapidly becoming a hell in every part of the world. In cities more than anywhere else, people feel lonely, unwanted, and afraid. The questions echo in empty hearts: "Where do I belong? Where is my place?"

Modern civilization, with all of its technological advances, is supposed to make us feel more comfortable and at home. It hasn't worked that way; almost the exact opposite has happened. We feel less comfortable and less at home than ever before. In former times, things were simpler and the questions asked less, but now things change so quickly it is almost deadening. More and more people live in mobile homes. People change jobs, jobs change people. Children find it difficult to make and keep friends, often because they're not in one place long enough to do so. Many mothers are not sure whether they should be out working to help the family financially or whether their place is in the home providing a haven to which other members of the family can return after working and studying. Fathers work hard, and wonder whether they'll be working tomorrow. Everything changes so rapidly that children begin to wonder whether they really occupy a place in the hearts of their mixed-up parents. We all kind of wonder where *do* we belong?

We can land on the moon, but we wonder whether the air on earth will be breathable next year, whether our waters will be drinkable, whether we will be smothered by our own wastes.

Things are changing in the world, and the fear of Cain is coming

31

out more clearly than ever before. There is a pervasive sense of being victimized. There is boredom and a feeling of helplessness, and acute anxiety causes us to cry out "Where do we belong? Where is our place?"

The question is a healthy one because it shows that at least we know something is wrong, that we're in trouble. It's a lot better to ask the question than simply complain about our destiny, feel sorry for ourselves, and feel bitter toward God and our fellowmen. And there *is* an answer.

We do have a place to find salvation, and we have the word of God to guide us there. God is seeking out those of us who are lost and He has a place prepared and waiting. The cross of Jesus marks the spot and shows that God is alive and He has a place for us.

If we read the story of Cain correctly, we see that he had no interest in repenting and returning to God. He wanted to continue in his own way, even though it meant bearing the mark of a fugitive and a wanderer. Cain went away from the presence of the Lord to wander in the land of Nod, east of Eden, and he never found his place.

God has a place for us, a place with Him. We can find it by turning to Him in repentance and faith. It is a remarkable place He summons us to. A cross outside a city wall where Jesus, His Son, gave His life for all of us. God made that place, and it is our place.

St. Paul tells us that when Jesus died, all died. We see ourselves there on the cross of Jesus. He died for all, and He died for us. That is a real place, a good place, the place of salvation.

Salvation comes only through Jesus. That is God's doing and there is nothing we can do to save ourselves. God has the place of forgiveness and that place is the cross of Jesus where He paid the price for our sins. Because of Him, for His sake, God forgives our every sin.

We must trust God that this is so. I have found the place. It is my place, our place. Jesus is our Savior. In Him there is forgiveness, in Him we finally come home. When we accept Jesus' forgiveness we have a new life. In Jesus we know we are sons and daughters of the Father. We leave the restlessness and the wandering behind. We take hold of Jesus by faith and live. In Him we begin our eternal life. This is eternal life, to know the Father, through the Spirit, in Jesus. This is Jesus' free gift to us, in our place. In Jesus we come home.

6

Whose Side Are We on?

But a samaritan, as he journeyed, came to where he was; and when he saw him, he had compassion, and went to him and bound up his wounds, pouring on oil and wine; then he set him on his own beast and brought him to an inn, and took care of him. (Luke 10:33-34 RSV)

There is an often-told story about a man coming along a road one day and running into another man who had been beaten and robbed. When the traveler saw the victim, he did something about it: "... he had compassion, and went to him and bound up his wounds, pouring on oil and wine; then he set him on his own beast and brought him to an inn, and took care of him."

Now a story like this usually rubs us the wrong way. We say: "This isn't the way things really happen." That's right, they don't usually happen that way.

In this same story that Jesus told, there are two other people mentioned, two pious churchmen. The first man noticed the victim, but managed to get by without becoming involved. "When he saw him, he passed by on the other side" (v.31). Then came the other churchman, and he also refused to get involved. When he saw the victim, he made believe he didn't see him and passed by occupied with his deep thoughts about God. Is that the way things really happen? Most of the time, yes they do. We come up with all kinds of "rational" and "intelligent" reasons for passing by. After all we really don't know the people who "seem" to need help and you can't trust anybody today, so better not get involved. We know they'll get help, from those responsible; family, friends, government agencies.

Helping people can get to be pretty expensive. Not only will it cost money, it also involves time. You can get into a lot of difficulty when you try to help people who are in trouble. It is not only the inconvenience, but the possibility of being held responsible for them. That's something we never plan to get into, something we never bargain for. But that's the kind of thing that really happens. It doesn't pay to help if you are going to get it in the neck because of it. Just because Jesus told this nice story about the Good Samaritan doesn't mean we have to go out and do the same thing.

Recently a book was written in which an author devoted time and effort to the question "Whose side are you on?" The answer he suggests when someone asks you that question today is: "Not yours, Mac." The best thing to do is to keep yourself free to avoid entanglements, to keep from being tied down either to a group or an individual. Don't tie yourself too tightly to anyone, so that you may be free to act in accord with your conscience, or desires or whims. The stated objective of this author was to encourage people to be free to join what he calls "the company of the compassionate," to be objectively concerned about other people, but not emotionally involved, for emotional involvement is a limitation. A lot of us may not understand the philosophy involved in these statements, but we are comfortable with the life style proposed: Be charitable, yes, but don't be ridiculous!

The occasion for the story Jesus told about the Good Samaritan was a question put to Him by a good churchman. The question he asked was, "Teacher, what shall I do to inherit eternal life?"

(v. 25). What he really was asking was, "Say, Jesus, whose side are you on?" Now Jesus was not about to be drawn into an argument about church politics, to be trapped into denying one thing by confirming another. He said to this biased theologian, "Your law, what does it say?" The man answered, "You shall love the Lord your God with all your heart, and with all your soul, and with all your strength, and with all your mind, and your neighbor as yourself" (v. 27). Jesus replied: "You have answered right, do this, and you will live" (v. 28).

When it came to debates, Jesus was a winner. He could stand up to anyone, and His answer to the tricky question won Him the argument. Even though He won the argument, He didn't mean, not for a minute, that any man, except himself, could fulfill that law completely. It is still true that if anybody could perfectly keep the law of God he would be saved, but it is also true that not one of us can do that.

The pious theologian knew that very well, so he asked Jesus a further question. "And who is my neighbor?" Jesus replied with the story of the Good Samaritan. It was a perfect but loving put-down to the less than earnest questioner and puts an important question to each of us: "Whose side are we on?" Are we on the side of Jesus? Before we say yes too quickly we'd better know what we're saying, because being on the side of Jesus takes a lot more than simple lip service. It takes straight thinking and practical action.

Whose side are we on? Being on the side of Jesus takes us into a whole new world, a world of compassion where simply *saying* we're concerned is not enough. What is said means nothing unless it is proved by what is done. Jesus is the Son of God and what He does shows that the one overpowering quality of God is compassion. He is a God of compassion, love, mercy and kindness. This living and loving God, the God of Abraham, Isaac, and Jacob, in compassion for us sent His Son to take on our whole human nature. In Jesus, God became a man, portraying through His life the compassionate love of God. Jesus can be approached by every man, and through Him every man can reach God. He himself tells us how we can come to God. Jesus said "No one comes to the Father, but by me" (John 14:6 RSV). Jesus is our brother, our Savior by His death on the cross and He is our Lord by His Resurrection.

Jesus called God "My Father" and told His disciples to pray "Our Father." Nobody calls God "My Father" in exactly the same way Jesus does, for that is something special. He is the eternal Son, not just another man but a man for all of us. When He died, He died for all. Since He has risen from the dead, He is Lord of all. By his Resurrection He has been declared to be the Son of God with power, both Lord and Christ. In Jesus, because of the forgiveness He won for us by His cross and in the exercise of faith that He is both Savior of the world and our personal Savior, we are able to say "Our Father." It is an evidence of the compassion of God that we, by faith in Jesus, can talk to God as "Our Father." When we say "Our Father" and mean it, we commit ourselves to be His sons and daughters. It is a commitment of faith in Jesus. It is a commitment to become like Jesus, to be with Him, to think with Him, to speak with Him, and to act with Him.

To act with Jesus—that is the problem. We want to *be* with Jesus, but are not willing to go so far as to *act* with Him. Actually, we don't want to think with Him either. That hurts, because attitude calls for action. As a man thinks in his heart, so he is (Prov. 23:7). What it really amounts to is that a lot of us admire Jesus, but we don't want to join Him in action. We need to remain free, so we think, free to be what we want to be. We want to be free without Jesus, whenever it is convenient for us to be without Him.

What price are we willing to pay to be on Jesus' side? Before we answer that, we had better realize that the price is high. The price is selfless compassion, like the Good Samaritan's, like Jesus.' It is the one thing that makes a man something like Jesus.

It is easy to imagine someone putting into words how most

people feel about this sort of thing: "Love of all mankind is church talk which never comes to grips with people as they really are. I give a lot of credit to anyone who can make a go of it. As for me, my heart contains much stubbornness that just can't get excited about the many unloved and unworthy people I know. So why pretend? There's that crude jerk I work with who deliberately needles me, that smooth liar who gets away with anything, that big wheel who thinks he's better than anyone else, that so-called 'friend' who took advantage of my trust and threw it in my face. By what magic am I supposed to feel anything but resentment, distrust, and a desire to just be left alone?" Now that seems to make a lot of sense. But does it?

The compassion that Jesus teaches is not just a feeling. Sure, we are fond of some people, and not so fond of others. Jesus never meant us to sit around trying to manufacture affectionate feelings for people who rub us the wrong way. It is not what we feel that counts, but rather what we *do* about these feelings. What is truly Christian is to be able to say, "As a matter of emotion, I dislike that person, but I will do good to him because Jesus loves him enough to have died for him. Jesus loves me, and I will love that person for Jesus' sake."

Love is not primarily something you feel, it is something you do. We don't know what the Good Samaritan felt, but we know what he did. Married couples don't always feel loving and tender toward each other, but they promise to act for one another until death. This is not a matter of mere emotion, it is a matter of doing, of action.

When we do something for someone out of love, it is amazing what can happen. Our usual formula "I am fond of that person, so I will help him" finds a new form, the compassion of Jesus himself, "I helped that person and now I am becoming fond of him."

Jesus calls for more than feelings; He commands compassion. At the Last Judgment He will not say: "I was hungry and you felt sorry for me, I was naked and you were embarrassed for me, I was in prison and you felt disgrace with me, I was sick and you were sympathetic?" No, He will say: "I was hungry and you gave me food, I was thirsty and you gave me drink, I was a stranger and you welcomed me, I was naked and you clothed me, I was sick and you visited me, I was in prison and you came to me" (Matt. 25:35,36 RSV).

We cannot merely tell one another which side we are on, we have to live it. Jesus says that. He says it to all of us who claim to be His followers but don't do anything about it. When Jesus asks, "Whose side are you on?" the answer will be found not in what we say, but in what we do.

7

The Lord Remembers Us

Be mindful of thy mercy, O LORD, and of thy steadfast love, for they have been from of old. Remember not the sins of my youth, or my transgressions; according to thy steadfast love remember me, for thy goodness' sake, O LORD! (Ps. 25:6,7 RSV)

Memory is a wonderful faculty of the mind. When we say "I remember," that memory helps us to do something better or to avoid something worse. It is human to remember, but the Psalmist said it can also be divine. He talked to God in a most human way when he said, "Be mindful of thy mercy, O LORD, and of thy steadfast love, for they have been from of old. Remember not the sins of my youth, or my transgressions; according to thy steadfast love remember me, for thy goodness' sake, O LORD!"

It is very human to talk to God. People who refuse to talk to God thereby refuse to be fully human. It is human to remember Him, and in that humanity of ours to appeal to Him, to ask His help, to beg His pardon, to accept His forgiveness, and to recognize that our lives do come from Him.

Why don't some people pray? Perhaps it is because they are not quite sure of God. They don't know how He really feels toward them, or they feel certain that He has it in for them. I think most of us can understand that attitude, because each one of us knows, deep down inside, that we have not done right by God. God exists, and if He does care, then He has every right to be displeased with each one of us. We are all human, we all have consciences, and we know that by ourselves we don't stand well with God. What right, then, does any one of us have to pray to God at all? What encouragement do we have to address Him as our loving Father? The encouragement is Jesus. Our right comes by way of Jesus. One might say, it is the reason for Jesus. By Him there is an access, a way of approach to the Father.

So there it is. Jesus came to be one of us. He was a man like us. But unlike us, He was a man who trusted altogether in His Father. In everything, He said, my Father and I are one. There is more to that statement than meets the eye. Jesus, the eternal Son of God our Father, came to be a man *for* us all. He took our place. He died for us. He lived and died with complete obedience to His Father and ours. For that, our Father and His gave Him a name that is above every name, that at the name of Jesus every knee should bow, every heart pray, every tongue confess that Jesus Christ is Lord to the glory of God our Father who arranged it all (Phil. 2:9-11). From Jesus I have learned to pray. In Him, I have forgiveness from God our Father, and anyone can have the same. I have accepted that forgiveness, all of us can do that too. In that acceptance, that faith, there is life and hope and confidence to pray.

In Jesus, I know God as my Father, with a heart for me something like the heart of my human father when he was alive My father wanted me to grow up to be a man and he disciplined me because he loved me. I could always go to him for help in any situation. That is the way God is. He is a Father. I know it in Jesus, His Son, and my Brother.

Do we have something on our minds, lying heavily on our hearts, holding us down or pulling us apart? Do we need help, and don't know where to turn? The Psalmist tells us where to turn: "Be mindful of your mercy, O Lord, and of your steadfast love. Remember us, Lord, remember us. Remember as you alone can.''

There would be little progress in our world if people could not remember. Automobile manufacturers can improve their product because of experience with previous models. Scientists build on what others did before them. They remember, and with that memory develop new and better ways of dealing with the problems of mankind, with disease, communications, transportation, and the other needs of everyday life.

Can we imagine what life would be without memory? If we couldn't remember the past, our childhood days, our intimate friendships? Memory can bring sadness. Sometimes we wish we could forget the past because some recollections bring back pain. If we could not remember, however, we might make the same mistakes over and over again.

For some of us, memory is just one way of building up resentment against those who have hurt us. These kinds of hurts are likely to stick in our memories longer than anything else. We may be among that large majority who are bitter over the way we were treated long ago. We are not ready to forgive all the hurts others have inflicted on us.

We have to be pretty sure of God to say to Him, "Remember me!" He could remember all the wrongs, all the hurt, all the insults, all the willfulness that makes us go our own way instead of His. It takes a lot of confidence in God to say to Him: "Remember me, O Lord. Remember not the sins of my youth, or my transgressions; according to your steadfast love remember me, for your goodness' sake, O Lord! Be mindful of your mercy and your steadfast love, for they have been from of old.''

We are funny creatures and we do things in very strange ways. We remember the faults of others, but we tend to forget our own. But the sins of our past, those of our youth, keep crowding in upon us. They keep coming up for review. Try as we will, we cannot put them out of our minds.

43

It doesn't do too much good to tell people to forget about their pasts. We can't forget. The memory, the guilt rising up from the past, haunts us and drives some of us to the point of insanity. If we can't tell people to forget, what can we do? A whole profession has arisen to help people rake up the past, to bring the whole business out into the open, in the hope that somehow they can arrive at an accommodation with their memories, their guilt, their attempt to wish the past out of existence.

The Psalmist didn't need a psychiatrist. He put it all right out in the open. Something great is written all over this prayer of his which asks God to remember him. That something the Bible calls repentance.

Repentance is the first step toward recovery. It is outright acceptance of God, His right to pass judgment, His displeasure at transgression of His will, His determination to impose judgment and His just penalties on those who ignore Him by going their own way. Repentance remembers God and it remembers sin. Without that recollection there would be no repentance. Repentance breaks the heart. It means being genuinely sorry for having offended God, being honestly and painfully aware of what our foolish and selfish behavior has done to a Father who loves. Now that's repentance and it's absolutely necessary for everyone who wants to be truly human.

Repentance remembers God, how He loves, how gracious He is, how good to forgive. Some people saw God for the first time that day when a cripple was brought to Jesus on a mat. Jesus said to him: "Take heart, my son, your sins are forgiven." It was not irrelevant then and it is not irrelevant now. It is the most relevant thing the Son of God could say to somebody in trouble: "Your sins are forgiven."

Because of Jesus, we can have this faith in God, that He forgives. Jesus died for all of us and paid the price of our sins. That is the heart of the gospel, the Good News, and on that Good News faith builds. Faith in Jesus is faith in God. Through faith in Jesus, we can accept the forgiveness of God for the past and start out each day with new courage, new hope, new joy. Every day becomes a new celebration, a celebration of God's mercy as we have it in Jesus.

The Psalmist said, "Remember me." Have faith in God. That's what it takes to have life in all its fulness. It means saying to God, "Father, you can do for me what I can't do for myself. I can't get rid of the past, but you can. If you forgive, I can live. For me, right now, be mindful of your mercy, Lord, and of your steadfast love, which have not failed in the past and will not fail me now. Remember not the sins of my life, nor my transgressions, by that steadfast love of yours, remember me . . . O Lord!"

That is the human way to talk to God. How else can we talk to Him? He wants us to come to Him in repentance and faith, and this is the way to do it: "Remember me, O Lord, forgive me, help me to live." He is God. He does remember. He doesn't need us to remind Him. Still, it is good for us to say it. "Remember me, O Lord, and forgive." It reminds us who we are and how much we need Him.

God knows who we are, we can't pull anything behind His back as students often do when teacher is not looking. His eyesight, His vision is perfect. He looks right into our inner beings. He sees not only what we have done, but the motives behind everything. He knows what we are and why. He remembers, and He forgives.

Why do some of us find it difficult to accept the forgiveness of God? It isn't that we don't believe that there is a God. We do. But some of us don't really "know" that God loves. We're not too sure about that. How will He take our repentance? Will it turn out to be just a useless exercise? The answer to these questions is in Jesus. I can't explain the Incarnation of Jesus, the mystery of His Redemption and His Resurrection to life again. But I can tell you this: He laid His life on the line for us. He died for us. He wasn't faking or playacting. His suffering was real and so was His death. In all of that, God was doing what only He can do. By the power of

45

God, Jesus was raised from the dead, and He is Lord of all. He has forgiveness for each of us. There is life for everyone who repents and has faith in Jesus.

Now that's something to celebrate. "You remember me, O Lord! You hear me, you respond to me, you forgive me my sins." He does remember us. We in turn try to remember Him. Christians all over the world set aside at least one day a week to remember the Lord in a special way. It isn't that they remember Him only that day nor is it done so much with a sense of obligation. It is a privilege. They say, "Let's make Sunday His day, because that's the day Jesus rose from the dead! It's a day to celebrate!"

Let's not just *go* to church. Let's enjoy the living beauty of God's mercy. Let it flood us and celebrate the glowing remembrance of it. Life in Jesus is joy. God gives us life in Him. Let's celebrate it in repentance and faith, in prayer and praise.

We all know that not everyday is going to be a tremendous mountaintop experience for us. But God gives us memory to recall His mercy, His goodness, His kindness so that we can celebrate the fact that the Lord remembers us.

8

Let Us Remember Him!

O give thanks to the Lord, for he is good, his steadfast love endures forever. Let Israel say, "His steadfast love endures forever." (Ps. 118: 1,2 RSV)

In the last chapter we investigated the prayer that said, "Remember us, God. Remember not our sins, remember your mercy and your steadfast love." We concluded by saying, "Remember God. Don't forget Him. Remember Him." The Psalmist remembered God and prayed to Him. There are a lot of us around who have forgotten how to pray to God. Where there is relative affluence, people seem to feel they don't need God. Yet many people who don't have to worry about where their next meal is coming from are bitter, dissatisfied, looking for something they seem unable to find.

Modern life has been described as pragmatic and profane and its persistent questions are these: "Does it work?" and "Does it count?" For the modern world, seeing is believing. One would think that such a practical and reasonable life style would bring happiness. But it doesn't. Life has become hurried, bleak, and frantic. Overburdened people try to reach somewhere and seem to get nowhere. For one thing there is a lack of time, the hours are too short, life is too short.

Even some churches have fallen into the trap. There is a lot of rushing, services scheduled to coincide with parking lot capacities, meetings, commissions, special activities, with little being accomplished. Spirituality seems shallow. Faith is a mere ethical piety, and the clergy are busy and restless. The proclamation of the word of God is sandwiched between fund-raising notices, social activities, and financial reports. Prayer becomes a nice prop, something on the scene, but not really necessary.

There are some people who ask whether men who ride jets and watch other men walking on the moon can still really believe in a God who has revealed himself in marvelous and miraculous ways. When faith is crucial, they doubt. Many young people, however, feel there's got to be something more to life than what science and technology have to offer, so they try almost anything in an attempt to find *the reality* behind "reality." They know instinctively that there has to be more meaning to life and they look for it in things like oriental religions, drugs, or the occult.

It is the way of desperation. Through despair some have come to find God, but despair itself has never done anything for anybody. I have seen some revel in despair, as if there were some kind of virtue about it. There is none. Despair is the road to meaningless existence and meaningless death.

What our world needs is faith. People sense that, but they shy away from faith in God. It is unfashionable to put one's faith in Him. It seems to deny a man his independence, his creativity, his manhood. That's how some have come to think in our time. We have come to believe the prophets of despair. Their preaching leads to only one end, and that is death, meaningless death.

The Bible is still *the* bestseller of all times. Why? Isn't it a sign that people are looking for something? Or better still, looking for *someone* in whom they can believe in whom they can put their trust, to whom they can entrust their very lives with complete confidence? That someone is God. He is not some vague force or merely the architect of the universe. He is the God who loves us so much He became one of us, in the person of Jesus of Nazareth.

All of it happened just as it is described in the Bible—directly, truthfully, without ornamentation or sentimentality. We don't have to read between the lines to find the real man. There He stands saying, "Blessed are the poor in spirit, for theirs is the kingdom of heaven." (Matt. 5:3). There He hangs on a cross and His voice calls out: "My God, my God, why did you abandon me?" (Matt. 27:46 TEV). That is Jesus Christ. In Him we see the mind and the heart of God.

One point should be clarified. The Father did not abandon Jesus and He does not abandon anyone who puts his trust in Him. That obedient Son, Jesus, was raised from the dead by the glory of His Father. He has been given a name that is above every other name that at the name of Jesus every knee should bow and every tongue confess that He is Lord to the glory of God the Father. Once more, in Jesus, God has shown himself to be a Father. He thinks, He feels, He cares, and He forgives. He restores, renews and gives life, as only He can. He provides the initiative for a new relationship between men and God, the relationship of faith. From our side it is faith, from His side it is faithfulness. He can be trusted, and He must be trusted. Trust is the key. It is what people are always looking for but seem unable to find.

It may come as a surprise to some today that God thinks, feels, and remembers. There is some of that surprise in this prayer: "God—you remember!" It is something like the surprise of a boy who thought of his father only as a disciplinarian, and suddenly discovered one day that his father really, truly, loved him. In that surprise is the beginning of trust and the start of a new relationship. On that day, the boy begins to be a man.

God is a gracious Father. People who know God have always said so. They are right. "The eternal purpose of God was realized in Christ Jesus our Lord," said St. Paul. "And in Him we have boldness and confidence of access through our faith in Him."

The Epistle to the Hebrews says, "Let us be bold to enter the sanctuary of God by the blood of Jesus. It is a new and living way He has opened up for us with the curtain of His own dying and rising to life again." Why? St. John said, "In this the love of God is made perfect within us, that we may have boldness in the day of judgment, because as He is so are we in this world."

Trust in God gives a person magnificent freedom. It sets him free from fear, from the anxieties that press him down, and from the horror of death. God is "tops" in the relationship of trust that is faith, because God comes through. He always come through. We can depend on it. With faith in Him, life becomes something more than constant dependence upon the pragmatic and profane. It gets a new quality and life begins anew.

God remembers. Since He remembers, prayer makes sense. We can lay our cards on the table with God, and He'll do the same with us. We can trust Him. It wasn't my idea that the world should come to know God through His word, it was His. I did not arrange it that God's Son should stand as the crossbearer for all mankind and as the risen Lord of all of history. God did that! I can't promise that I'll be with anybody "even until the end of the age." But Jesus does. He is called helper, comforter, savior, shepherd, healer, strength, light, guide, advocate, the way, the truth, and the life. I have never been able to say that my word, once uttered and dropped into the stream of history, would always come true, but Jesus does.

Faith in God is the beginning of our putting our complete trust in Him. Why, then, do some of us who claim to trust in God continue to moan and groan about our deficiencies, our lack of faith, our failure to persevere, and our smallness of vision? That's really thin sliced baloney, a lot of it. It is all part of a simpering, solacing attempt to put ourselves forward, with the insinuation that God must have fallen down somewhere. Picking through the rubble is not God's way of doing things. He scores all the time, but the falsely pious often fail to see it. That kind of piety isn't trusting. It doesn't take God seriously. It doesn't acknowledge Him as He is and doesn't expect Him to follow through as the God for whom all things are possible.

Who is going to program a solution for cleaning up the whole environment? Who can program and predict even the work of the church—its problems and opportunities—for the next ten years? Who can jump in with comprehensive solutions to war, drug abuse, broken families, generation gaps, divorce, racial tensions, and all the other human problems? Who can change a man's will, dissolve the deepness of his pride, and move him to believe the Good News of Jesus? Who can do that? God doesn't need people to do this *for* Him. We can't do anything *for* God, to improve His situation. We can only do the things that He wants done—*with* Him.

In God's household, nobody is a slave. All are sons and daughters. They are encouraged to be just like Him, bold "As He is, so we are in this world."

Through the contract God has closed with man by the death and Resurrection of His Son, by the presence of His Spirit, God lives in those who put their trust in Him. No longer slaves but sons, that's God's program. Pride goes out, faith comes in. Pride is killed in the death of Jesus, and faith is built on His Resurrection. God has not called us to be clods, but responsible sons and daughters in His family. He accepts responsibility for us, and we must accept Him, only Him.

The Psalmist accepted God. "God," he said, "You remember. Remember not the sins of my youth, but remember your mercy, O Lord, and your steadfast love. . . ."

We don't have to remind God. He doesn't need reminders. He is thinking all the time and feeling. If someone is in trouble, God feels it. If someone hurts, He feels it; if someone worries, He feels it; and if someone dies, He feels that, too. God's feeling is mercy, and it is steadfast love. He keeps on giving and forgiving. He never gives up.

That is how God is. It may not be exactly the way we've heard it,

51

but that's how He is. It may not be the way we've imagined Him to be, but that's the way He is. Our education and our experience may have caused us to think otherwise, but that's how He is.

Let us remember the Lord for He never forgets us!

9

Jesus Puts It All Together

He existed before all things, and in union with him all
things have their proper place. (Colossians 1:17 TEV)

In one of those big, encompassing, and deeply theological
statements with which St. Paul used to begin his letters, there is
this remarkable statement about Jesus: "He existed before all
things, and in union with Him all things have their proper place."

Almost everyone agrees that the world is mixed up and it seems
daily to get worse. There is hardly anything in which there are not
violent and hard differences of opinion, and there are many groups
of people holding these opinions in inflexible opposition to others.
To be any kind of executive—political, ecclesiastical, or
business—must be very frustrating these days. It is getting to be
more difficult to put things together, to get people to work together
on something worthwhile without having it strain and break up in
front of your eyes.

It is like the situation in a lot of modern families. When the
children are younger, things can be kept more or less together.
Father goes to work, perhaps out of town, but eventually he comes
home and the whole family gathers around the dinner table to
become reacquainted, to catch up with things, and to get the feel of

each other again. It doesn't take very long, however, until things begin to change. One of the kids is in grammar school, another is in high school, another is in college. One of the kids stays at a friend's house for supper, another has to stay in school for play practice, and Mom has an early meeting of her own. Dad comes home from work to find himself alone, with dinner being kept warm on the stove. He opens the mail and finds a letter from the kid in college asking for money. On the family bulletin board he finds three notes, one asking him to feed the dog, another asking him to pick up his son who stayed at his friend's house for supper, and another asking him to pick up the daughter at school after play practice. He also finds a scribble from his wife saying she'll be home later after her Christian housewives' meeting. It just so happens tonight he had planned to get through that extra work he needs on the job tomorrow. Things can get pretty complicated and mixed up.

Modern society is getting to be like a gigantic jigsaw puzzle. Trying to put things together and keeping things that are together from falling apart has become an almost impossible task. Politics has become a jungle. Teachers go on strikes, parents want less and less to do with their children, policemen and firemen want more and equal pay, unions and management are always at each other's throats, blacks and whites don't trust each other. The poor demand to be taken care of and the middle class resists paying the bill, the rich get away with murder and the poor languish in prisons for minor crimes. That's the way things are. In almost every modern country the pieces are falling apart.

These things just can't be swept under the rug; that will solve nothing. Somebody must begin to clean things up or it will overwhelm all of us; but nobody seems to know exactly how. But, as bad as it is, the situation is not hopeless. If it depended on you or me, it would be hopeless. If it depended on the politicians, capitalist or Communist, it would be hopeless. If it depended on all the church people in the world, with all their piety and great pronouncements and programs, it would still be hopeless. There is only one hope for the world, only one who can put it all together again. He is the one St. Paul was talking about. "He existed before all things, and in union with Him all things have their proper place."

To many people, Christian or not, that will sound like plain nonsense. It sounded like nonsense when St. Paul first said it to the Roman world, which had already begun to fall to pieces.

Jesus Christ came with the Good News, the Good news that God who made this world of ours, who put it together in the first place, can and will put it together again. Jesus did not just bring a message from the Father. He took all of our sins, selfishness, and guilt and had it nailed with Him on the cross.

Jesus was crucified on a hill outside of Jerusalem. He died for the sins of the world. Something happened there on that cross that touches us all. St. Paul tells us what. "God made peace through his Son's death on the cross, and so brought back to himself all things, both on earth and in heaven."

During this twentieth century, some people got the idea that maybe the nations of the world could finally get together and make this planet a better place for people to live on. With the development of rapid communication and transportation, there seemed to be a chance, a greater chance than before, of understanding and peace. Science and education were going to help in the development of a new order where people would be able to do their thing and be at peace. They would patch up their differences without war and happiness and justice would prevail.

We all know how things have worked out. More money is being spent on armaments today than at any time in the history of the world. Every little crisis in international affairs makes people shake in their boots because this might be the one that will be the beginning of the end. There are more antagonisms, hatred, jealousies, and envy around today than ever before. Nations with centuries of history are falling apart at the seams. The same thing is happening to institutions within those nations. They simply can't hack it. They can't solve the problems of mankind and people are beginning to see it.

Where do we go from here? Into oblivion or into a jungle where we just chew each other up? In a lot of places that's actually what is happening. We see it in the world and shamefully we see it even in the churches. In every case, it happens when people forget the God who put things together in the first place, and who will have to put them together again if life is to make any sense at all.

God, our Father, is ready and willing. If that is true, that's really good news. How can we be sure that it *is* true? In the same way St. Paul did. For the first followers of Christ, the Good News was real. It had to be real, because Jesus is not only a *real* man, but the *real* God. They knew Him firsthand. They saw Him die. They met Him alive again. To these men and women, Jesus was no dream figure as He has become to many people today, both inside and outside the churches. They knew Him, and things began to fall into place again.

"Christ is the visible likeness of the invisible God," St. Paul said. "He is the firstborn Son, superior to all created things. For by him God created everything in heaven and on earth, the seen and the unseen things, including spiritual powers, lords, rulers and authorities. God created the whole universe through him and for him. He existed before all things, and in union with him all things have their proper place" (Col. 1:15-17 TEV).

In union with Him, by faith in Him, with trust in Him, that is the secret that God shared with all who will believe. I can know it, and you can, in union with Jesus. With Jesus the whole puzzle of life begins to take form and to make sense.

Our universe did not come into existence by chance. It is not the result of blind gropings by unconscious forces. It did not come about by some dark blob of lifelessness somehow evolving into life. Our universe is the purposeful creation of a God with mind and heart. Those are human terms, but it is the way the Bible describes Him.

The mind of the God who put things together in the first place makes sense, but only when we "get with" Him, when we begin to see what He has in mind and stop trying to impose on Him what *we* have in mind. That may shock some of our sensibilities, especially if we're very impressed with ourselves and put great importance on our own little thoughts. It may also come as a shock to realize we can go our own independent ways and go to hell in the process. If we want to know something about what hell is like, all we have to do is take a good look at our world today. People, young and old, make a terrible mess of their lives. In the process they embitter, damage, and wreck the lives of others around them. I don't have to argue about hell; its evidence is all around us. Only God sees it as it is. He has the picture of what once was and what can be again. The whole picture is what He had in mind when He sent us His Son. By that Son He put things together in the first place and by that Son He has made His move to put things together again.

The first step the Son took was to make things good again by His death, to pay the price for us, to reconcile to the Father all things in heaven and on earth. There is nothing provincial about Jesus. He is the cosmic Redeemer, the Savior in every sense of the word. There have been other men who some people call "saviors of mankind," but they don't come anywhere close to Jesus, who died and rose again. That puts Him in a class all by himself. He existed before all things. He went the way of every man, that each one of us might have forgiveness and life in His name. "He is the firstborn Son who was raised from death, in order that he alone might have the first place in all things. For it was by God's own decision that the Son has in himself the full nature of God. Through the Son, then, God decided to bring the whole universe back to himself. God made peace through his Son's death on the cross, and so brought back to himself all things, both on earth and in heaven" (Col. 1:18-20 TEV).

Jesus Christ existed before all things. When we are in union with Him, when we trust Him and follow Him, all things begin to take their proper place again. We can then become men and women as we were intended to be. With faith in Him, we can learn to love again, and to be truly and fully human. It is a reversal of most of the stuff we are being sold by the world today, but that is the way it is in union with Jesus.

With Jesus, life begins to make sense. Forgiveness from the Father in Jesus makes life worth living. The new attitudes and dispositions that come with experienced forgiveness from the Father make life new. The actions to which we are impelled by faith in Christ make love a reality. It is a new beginning, a new birth. It is the kind of things some people are trying to achieve today with drugs, alcohol, and "liberated" sex, but they will never find it that way. It is only in Jesus, in union with Him, that things fall into place so that we can put it together. It is what the Bible calls salvation and being filled with the Spirit. It is life and health. Jesus puts people and things together again. "If any one is in Christ, he is a new creation" (2 Cor. 5:17 RSV).

10

The Whole Picture

The grace of the Lord Jesus Christ and the love of God and the fellowship of the Holy Spirit be with you all. (2 Cor. 13:14 RSV).

The Psalmist wrote: "The earth is the LORD's and the fulness thereof, the world and those who dwell therein" (Ps. 24:1 RSV).

Even if we are people with eyes toward the Lord, we still have to be aware of the fact that the earth is becoming covered with all kinds of trash. We worry about the quality of our food and at the same time we are in danger of being buried with our garbage. We have all read the sign "Every litter bit hurts," and it's time to do something about it. If we are conscious and aware that "the earth is the Lord's," then ecology should be one of our real concerns. Part of our problem has been that we have come to regard the earth—the sea, the sky, the land—as our own possessions, to do with as we please. Now we're learning rather dramatically that we are only tenants on an earth in which God is the owner.

It is interesting that the word "ecology," which is used to describe the relationship of man to his total environment—the seas, wild and domestic life, cities and country side and all that surrounds us—comes from a Greek word that means "house."

Ecology is the study of a house. All the articles, books, legislation, speeches, and talk about ecology won't change a thing. We won't change, until we realize it's God's house, and we're living in it by His grace. "The earth is the Lord's and the fulness thereof, the world and those who dwell therein."

We are told that the basic problem we have is the production of goods, some necessary and some not so necessary, for a world population growing by leaps and bounds. Jesus said, "Man's life does not consist in the abundance of things that he possesses." But we have gone ahead on the assumption that a man's life does indeed consist in the abundance of things he possesses. We produce more and more things, all of which wear out and are discarded. But now we don't know how to get rid of the discards. Almost all of the pollution in the world today is the result of our efforts to improve the lot of mankind. We wanted better transportation and the automobile was invented. Now it has become the major source of the air pollution affecting everyone's health and safety.

Nothing is really going to change in this world of ours until we begin to change. For a long time it was thought that we could go right on doing what we were doing and everything would be all right. Now we see that it is absolutely necessary that we change our attitudes toward the world in which we live or we'll destroy ourselves and it too. There are some pessimists around who say that people are just going to destroy themselves eventually, and nothing can be done about it. If I thought that, I wouldn't bother putting this book together. People can change. It takes some effort, but it is possible. The first step in the process of change for anyone is to recognize that God is the Lord. This is one thing millions of people just don't want to admit to themselves. If they did, they would have to change, and we don't like to change. When it comes right down to it, we don't even like to hear about God; God-talk makes us uncomfortable, and we prefer being comfortable.

If it's true that the earth is the Lord's then we had better get used to the idea that we have to live with Him. If we ignore His lordship over the world, we get what we have now: people directly and indirectly killing each other off. The cities are one of man's most magnificent creations, but they have become deathtraps, covered by smoke and smog. Pollution has drifted even into the countryside, poisoning our water and food. Science and technology are not going to change. And we won't change until we come to terms with the idea that we have to live with God, for the earth is His and those who dwell therein.

How does anyone come to terms with God? The first step is repentance. The Bible repeats that over and over, but not too many listen. Repentance means turning from our way to God's way. It means turning away from ourselves to God, coming around and doing things differently, making good what we've done wrong, coming across with faith, the kind of faith that says He knows what He is doing, that He loves us, is able to forgive our past, and can give us new life if we trust Him and follow Him. Solving our problem won't be just a matter of putting our heads together to find a solution. We must change from within, where the Holy Spirit does His work. Our spirits must be changed because they are befouled with hatred, jealousy, fear, brutality, and a desire to dominate others. Our spirit is shortsighted, characterized by a narrow egotism that is making our world uninhabitable. We engage in wars to destroy one another and make the world safe for ourselves, but that doesn't work. We must live with each other, and the only way we can live with each other is to live with God in repentance and faith. That is becoming clearer every day.

What we think of as the whole picture, our view of life, what we think about our origin, purpose and destiny, what we regard as the most important facts of life, will determine who we are and if we really believe that "the earth is the Lord's . . . and those who dwell therein."

Who is this Lord who controls the universe, determines boundaries, and keeps all in existence? The Bible tells us that He is kind and loving, that He continues to love even when His creatures reject Him. It is in His name that St. Paul sent the greetings, "the grace of our Lord Jesus Christ, and the love of God, and the fellowship of the Holy Spirit be with you all."

The grace of our Lord Jesus Christ is the grace of God. "The grace of God has appeared for the salvation of all men." His grace appears today in Jesus of whom was said, "We saw Him, we talked to Him, we felt Him with our hands. We had with us the Lord of life. We saw His glory, the glory as of the only begotten of the Father, full of grace and truth."

The fact that Jesus came and became a man means that God thinks men are worth saving. We may go our own way, but He still thinks so. He still keeps offering His grace to the world, in Jesus. A recent book blasted mankind with the charge that we're all apes. God doesn't think so; He wants to save us by His grace. He sent His Son to become one of us and that Son died on a horrible cross to pay the price for our forgiveness. That forgiveness is still there for the asking. "The grace of our Lord Jesus Christ be with you."

The love of God be with you. "God so loved the world that he gave his only begotten Son that whosoever believeth in him should not perish but have everlasting life" (John 3:16). It takes faith to believe that, and that's what it takes to be a person living with God whose world this is. In Jesus, God makes sense to us; when God makes sense, the world begins to make sense again. When the world makes sense to a man, he begins to live again. Our world needs the love of God; there is nothing it needs more. When we finally come to see that God loves us, we change. Our world needs to be changed and this is the only way, through God's love in Jesus.

Even after all the tribulation and distress, the nakedness and famine, the peril, persecution and the sword, St. Paul still trusted in the cross of Jesus: "If God be for us, who can be against us? He that spared not his own Son, but delivered him up for us all, how shall he not with him also freely give us all things?" (Rom.

8:31,32). Faith in the goodness and generosity of God returns hope to our hearts and with hope, we can change; without it, we can't live.

God's Word came to the world in its creation, it came again in the person of Jesus, and it comes today through His Holy Spirit. The Spirit inspires the Good News of Jesus bearing the love of the Father. By the Good News, the Holy Spirit produces a new fellowship, a new relationship between people, a revival of life.

A new dream has been born, wrought by the Holy Spirit, a dream becoming a reality of men living for God and in fellowship with one another. A new kind of community is emerging, the fellowship of the Holy Spirit.

St. Peter talked about the coming of the Spirit when he quoted Joel in his Pentecost sermon: "In the last days it shall be, God declares, that I will pour out my Spirit upon all flesh, and your sons and your daughters shall prophesy, and your young men shall see visions, and your old men shall dream dreams" (Acts 2:17 RSV).

That new dream began to take shape in reality by the power of the Holy Spirit on Pentecost, and we are living in times when we are witnessing the fulfillment of the promise as evidenced by the charismatic renewal and the formation of New Testament communities. This is the dream of complete salvation, a dream that is coming true. There is hope for here and now, and for tomorrow.

Ecology has become an unhappy synonym for survival of the human race. What we need is not merely survival, but salvation. A scientist has said: "More science and more technology are not going to get us out of the present ecologic crisis until we find a new religion, or rethink our old one." This is a religious crisis. It is a crisis of man, and man is not really man until he sees himself as part of God's world. Man is not really man until he knows God and learns to live with God in repentance and faith. The world will not be saved until men are changed by faith in the living God, faith that enables a man to see the whole picture and to put things in their place. "The grace of our Lord Jesus Christ, the love of God, and the fellowship of the Holy Spirit be with you all."

11

Suppose We Goof?

Some time later Paul said to Barnabas, "Let us go back and visit our brothers in every city where we preached the word of the Lord, and find out how they are getting along." Barnabas wanted to take John Mark with them, but Paul did not think it was right to take him, because he had not stayed with them to the end of their mission, but had turned back and left them in Pamphylia. They had a sharp argument between them, and separated from each other. Barnabas took Mark and sailed off for Cyprus, while Paul chose Silas and left, commended by the brothers to the care of the Lord's grace. He went through Syria and Cilicia, strengthening the churches. (Acts 15:36-41 TEV)

Only Luke is with me. Get Mark and bring him with you, because he can help me in the work. (2 Tim. 4:11 TEV)

The Scripture quoted above gives the clue to answer the question, "Suppose we goof?" If it weren't for the fact that we can get another chance in life, the name of Mark would not hold the honor it does among Christians today. Thank God! There is the possibility of another chance in life, even if we goof badly.

The Scripture account in Acts 15:36-41, began in the city of Antioch, the city where the name "Christian" was first used to describe the followers of Jesus. Paul and Barnabas arrived there after a grueling but satisfying trip to the cities of Asia Minor where they had to tell people about Jesus, and where the Good News had been well received. After a period of rest in Antioch, Paul suggested to Barnabas that they return to the cities they had evangelized and check on their progress. Barnabas wanted to take John Mark with them, but Paul objected because John Mark hadn't completed the original mission with them. As men will, the two disagreed, and decided to go off on their own with their chosen companions.

John Mark was not only a dropout, but he broke up what had been a beautiful friendship. The young man had washed out at a crucial time and Paul was afraid he might do the same again. Later on, as we know, things changed, and this same John Mark wrote the second book of the New Testament.

The story of John Mark's youthful instability was recorded in the Book of Acts by St. Luke, an associate of St. Paul. Luke makes no attempt to excuse Paul for refusing to take John Mark along on the second journey. If Paul had his reasons, that was enough. Barnabas thought that young John Mark should be given another chance, and he was willing to go it with him alone if necessary. Barnabas must have known he was taking a risk, that the same thing could happen again, but he decided to give him another chance anyway. Maybe Barnabas himself knew personally what another chance can mean when one has goofed. It took a lot to do what he did, but he stood his ground.

The same John Mark seems to have been at the scene the night Jesus was captured before His crucifixion. He is the only one who tells the story about a certain teenager who followed Jesus as He was led away captive. One of the soldiers saw the boy hanging around and grabbed for him. The boy ran, but not before the soldier had torn the clothing right off his back. The boy got away stark naked, accompanied by the laughter of the soldiers. It is possible that John Mark was that boy and it is possible that Barnabas knew about it.

During the forty days after the Lord's Resurrection when He visibly appeared to His followers and commissioned them to preach the Good News to the whole world, it is very possible that young John Mark was present. Mark was in on the founding of the church at Pentecost, and he was an integral part of its early life.

Barnabas couldn't forget that. Barnabas himself was a strong man, and a kind man, a mature man, a spirit-filled minister of the Gospel—he was not a party hack, a political creature, but a man totally committed to Jesus.

John Mark had been chosen to help Paul and Barnabas in the work of carrying the Good News, but somewhere along the line he lost heart and walked out on the job. We don't know exactly what happened, but life isn't all glory, especially when you are telling the Good News of Jesus. There was a lot of trouble, opposition, and violence along the way. Maybe this frightened and discouraged the young man, and so he copped out.

Paul and Barnabas were both disappointed; but when the time came for them to return to the cities they had evangelized to encourage the people there in the faith, Barnabas suggested they take John Mark with them because he still believed in the boy. Paul disagreed. We can only guess at how Paul might have felt. He probably didn't have anything against the boy, but he just didn't want him along on this trip. Barnabas did because maybe he saw something in the young man that Paul couldn't see. Two strong Christian men can disagree, even to the point of going their own way. Neither lost faith in Jesus, but they were very human men who decided not to allow their disagreement to become an issue disrupting the whole Christian community. Paul took Silas, Barnabas took Mark, and all four went their way, continuing their labors for Jesus.

We should find this incident rather comforting. When we see people fighting with each other in the church, we could easily lose heart. Most of the time they fight about things that have no relationship to important issues. Sometimes there are very human struggles for power, which are understandable in human circumstances, but distressing, because the enemies of Jesus exploit that kind of stuff. Failure and weakness are not unknown in the church, which is probably why people are in the church. They need a Savior and forgiveness just as much as those outside the church. Two great people like Paul and Barnabas could have a genuine falling-out, and still go Jesus' way, not as self-righteous prigs but as sinners forgiven by the grace of God in Jesus.

We all need and have the forgiveness of Jesus. We can all have the new life that is received by repentance and faith in Him. Where there is weakness, in Him there is strength. Where there is failure, in Him there is renewal of hope, joy, patience, kindness, humility and self-control. It is the continuing labor of the Holy Spirit to give people like us a new chance for a new beginning.

John Mark was given another chance, even though he failed his first real test. All of us, young or old, fail like that today, and we all get another chance. Barnabas took John Mark with him to Cyprus, and some years went by. We can only guess at what happened during those years, for the early Christians did not play up their exploits or parade their piety. They went their way with Jesus as if it were the most natural thing to do in the whole world. Barnabas took Mark along on that mission to Cyprus, and Mark stayed with it. Barnabas was proved right. The young man had a lot more in him than could be seen on the surface. What he had was faith in Jesus, and faith in Jesus is the victory that overcomes. Faith overcomes failure, just as love covers a multitude of defects. That kind of faith is durable enough to give someone all the chances they need.

There is only one person in this world who never needed another chance. He went right out to do whatever He had to, and did it. What is more, He did what He had to do with complete confidence in His Father that everything would turn out all right. Things did not look very good the day He carried His cross to Calvary, but He was confident it would end well, and it did.

God is in control, and there is always room for faith. No matter what we have done or how far we have fallen, there is always Jesus. He took the big chance for us; He died for us, and He paid the price we would have to pay. There is forgiveness, another chance in Jesus, no matter how we goof. I know that is true; I know it for myself. It takes faith to go with Jesus, but He is the way. He is the way, by faith, from failure to a new future. In Him we have another chance, not to prove ourselves, but another chance for a new life that brings hope every day.

Even with St. Paul, John Mark had another chance. When he was in Rome near the end of his life, he wrote to Timothy and said, "Get Mark, and bring him with you, because he can help me in the work" (2 Tim. 4:11 TEV). Paul had heard about Mark's faithfulness and he wasn't about to stand on any feeling of past personal injury. Paul was too big a man for that. And Mark was too big a man to refuse to come. A big man knows what it means to have another chance, and doesn't waste time trying to prove to others that he did it all himself. The big man recognizes kindness when he sees it, and is grateful for it. Life is too short for smallness, for the narrowness and bitterness of spirit which refuses to see and accept the grace of God as it comes to people like ourselves, who find out for themselves how great the kindness of God really is.

The grace of God changes things and people. If it were not for the grace of God, people would never change. All of life would just be a constant clawing to get ahead, without any hope for the future. The grace of God works to make people over, to strengthen what is weak and to right what is wrong. The grace of God is not just pious talk. It is real, it works, it changes people and it gives life. By the grace of God, people are forgiven and learn to forgive. By the grace of God, Jesus died for us and rose again. By the grace of God, there is another chance for us even if we goof badly. By

God's grace and love, He has room in His heart for you and me, to take our smallness and make us big, to open our eyes so that we can see, to overcome our weakness, whatever it is, and to give us strength to live.

The grace of God speaks to us in Jesus. "Him that comes to me, I will never turn away." He will give us all the chances we need. He is not like us who say, "He had his chance, and now it's too late!" The Good News of God is forgiveness, it is: "Come. Don't stay away until you've proved yourself. Come right now. You have another chance." The least we can do is to try to forgive others as He forgives us because we all need another chance.

PART II

WHERE LIES THE WAY?

12

Jesus Is the Way

Jesus said to him, "I am the way, and the truth, and the life; no one comes to the Father, but by me." (John 14:6 RSV)

The Scriptures say: "Train up a child in the way he should go, and when he is old he will not depart from it" (Prov. 22:6 RSV).

Old-fashioned as it may sound, starting out a boy on the right road has for years been pushed pretty hard by educators and psychologists. Many of them declare the first few days or the first few months after a child's birth are very crucial and the first few years of his life are the truly formative ones.

This fact was noticed long before the advance of child psychology and those who wanted to dominate the lives of other people took advantage of it. Hitler knew what he was doing with his youth corps. Communist regimes throughout the world have long been aware of the fact, and always give a lot of time and attention to the young. Perhaps they are not always successful, because young people do have minds of their own, but they try very hard to get them programmed for life.

Start out children on the right road and you will have them for the rest of your lives. There is not too much argument about that. The argument begins when we start asking, "Which is the right road?"

We have a lot of talk in the Western world about giving young people the tools of democracy, and it is not just useless talk. Young people need to be educated to become responsible citizens of the countries in which they live, able to think for themselves, able to talk intelligently, and able to act with regard for the rights of others. How do we get young people to think, to talk, and to act as responsible citizens? Obviously, a great deal of education has not been successful in achieving that objective. Instead of blaming the educators, we ought, instead, to take a good look at ourselves. We can't educate young people to live in a dream world when the real world looks altogether different. The real world, for the most part, is the one older people have created. It is a world of advanced technology with mass production of cars, electricity, electronic marvels, household gadgets, nuclear power, and jet transportation which makes all previous ages look almost like the Stone Age. We have done all that, but where are we going? Do we know? Does anybody know? If anybody knows, can they tell us how to get there?

A lot of people can tell us what is wrong with the world, but only one man in all of history ever claimed to have the complete answer for the young and the old, the answer as regards the way to go. Which is the right way? Jesus said, "I am the way, the truth, and the life."

That answer won't make a lot of sense to many people today, because it doesn't fit their life styles, their ways of thinking, talking and acting. For some strange reason, a lot of these people have the idea that Jesus is out of date. But who, really, is out of date? A long time ago Jesus said, "A man's life does not consist in the abundance of things he possesses." Psychologists are telling us the same thing today. I wouldn't be at all surprised that someone reading this message today would like to be that big, brawny football star, would like to go the way of that handsome guy who throws all those great passes and has all those beautiful babes hanging around him. I once saw one of those superstars interviewed on television and I don't think I've ever seen a more lonely or restless man in my life.

There are girls who see themselves on the stage at Atlantic City under the lights, holding the roses and wearing the crown of Miss America and getting the attention of the world. Being in the contest doesn't mean a girl is going to turn out badly, but it takes an awful lot of character to overcome the temporary adulation, the quick success and the quick oblivion, not to mention the personal exploitation that goes with the whole business.

Others see themselves in dark-paneled offices, dressed in expensive suits, busy phones on the desk, reaping big profits. Along with that dream goes the other one of the perfect hostess with the mostest, the wife of the successful executive, giving swinging parties that are the talk of the season. People who have tried to find the ultimate in life that way can tell us from firsthand experience that if that's all there is to it, it isn't worth it.

Some see themselves in the ivory tower of academic life looking down disdainfully on the ebb and flow of history, commenting on the faults of men and of societies. Others are not attracted by that at all; they see themselves as gone—completely out of it—on a trip so to speak. It is just too horrible to belong to the real world at all, so they "cop out" entirely.

A few years ago everyone was singing a song entitled, "I've Got to Be Me." That's right. We can't be someone else, we have to be ourselves. We must find ourselves beneath all the self-delusion, self-satisfaction, and self-deception that most of us cover ourselves with. That's precisely the problem. How do we get there, anyway?

Jesus says, "I am the way." If anybody else but Jesus would say that to me, I would say he was deceiving himself. If it were anybody but Jesus, he would be doing just that.

I write this message for the sake of Jesus. I am compelled to write about Him and talk about Him because He expects that of anyone who claims to follow Him. That is really how we can tell the men from the boys, the ones who really know Him from those who just think they know Him. Jesus' men and women think enough of Him to tell others about Him.

This is not a matter of age or special vocation either. There are boys and girls who are the best evangelists around because they speak quite naturally about Jesus. They are perfectly willing to tell others about Him. They know Him, and in their own way have made up their minds to follow Him. They found Him, and in finding Him they found themselves. They are on the way, the right way, His way.

Someone once said. "There are many things in the Bible that bother me. It is not the things I can't understand that bother me; it's the things I do understand." There is no mistaking the meaning of Jesus; He said He was the way, and He meant the only way. No man comes to the Father, He said, but by Me. No one really gets to know God, understanding how He feels and what His intentions are, except by Jesus Christ. Anybody can understand that. They may not agree, but it can be understood because it's what Jesus said.

Medical science informs us that a person deprived of oxygen for four minutes will suffer irreversible brain damage. The truth of that statement does not depend on whether we agree with it or not because it is a matter of fact that if there is no oxygen the brain cells will be damaged beyond repair. There is no substitute for oxygen, and a difference of opinion will make no difference at all about that. Jesus was just as uncompromising when He said, "I am the way." There is no substitute for His self-giving humanity, no substitute for His atoning blood, no substitute for His resurrection to put things right.

There are some people who would come back at me with the suggestion that some truth can be found in all religions. That's not a comeback because it is completely irrelevant. There is some truth both in philosophy and science, but none of these truths can

76

substitute for Jesus Christ. There is no substitute for Him. He says, "I am the way."

Jesus is the way to God, to the heart of God, to the Father. He is not just *one* way. He is the *only* way. No man comes to the Father, He says, except by Me. That is about as uncompromising as you can get. The durable quality and the sharp edge of the gospel, the Good News, is in Jesus himself, in no one else and in nothing else.

What is it like to go that way? It is learning faith in Jesus, accepting forgiveness in Jesus, enjoying life in Jesus, going with Jesus. That is the way, the only way, the one for the young to take if they are going to find fulfillment, and the one for the older to follow to find their destiny. Jesus is the only way.

The early Christians were very much impressed by this statement of the Lord. They referred to themselves as followers of "the Way." They didn't mind being known as the Jesus people, any more than Jesus minded being known as the Savior of all people everywhere, even though this road took Him to the cross; that was His way and He accepted it willingly because it came from His Father. He went His Father's way, obediently, always the faithful Son, and He took whatever it brought Him, including the death of a common criminal. "Who for the joy that was set before him endured the cross, despising the shame, and is set down at the right hand of the throne of God" (Heb. 12:2). Death was not the end of Him. The end, as we now see and understand, was His Resurrection. Jesus Christ rules, Jesus Christ is Lord. From anyone else's mouth it might sound arrogant, from His it does not. "I am the way," He says.

We often hear people say, "I don't care what religion a man has as long as he lives right." There is a good deal of piety in that statement, a sort of secular piety. It sounds almost holy; the fact is, that it is pure nonsense. Breathing won't do us any good at all unless we have oxygen to breathe. Some may try carbon monoxide to solve their problems like some young people who claim to find religious experience in mind-blowing drugs, or some older people who try to escape from their problems and the harsh realities of life with alcohol or frenzied sexual activity. That doesn't solve anything and it only makes things worse. There is no truth and no life in it. If we are looking for truth to light the way, to give meaning to life, this is the way—Jesus.

Dreams vanish and plans crumble. Muscular bodies and sharp brains succumb to the pressures of time. Beauty fades like flowers. Success is like gelatin, hard to get hold of and it doesn't last. At the end of the road there is a wasteland holding no promise for tomorrow. To have hope and be saved from all that, there is a way. "I am the way," Jesus said.

Jesus is redemption and He is reconciliation. He is forgiveness and He is life. He is Resurrection and He is the promise of a new tomorrow. He is the way. That is why I have to tell about Him. It's why I write, preach, and teach. It is the reason for my work. He is our only hope and He says, "I am the way."

I will concede that going His way, especially at first, feels very strange. It's difficult to fill the mold. It's something like a kid trying on a new suit. The shoulders are too broad, the sleeves too long, the pants too wide. It's all a little uncomfortable, but the accompanying parent usually says, "Wrap it up; he'll grow into it." And that is exactly what happens. He grows into it. That is the way it is with Jesus. When we come to follow Him, we begin to grow. Day by day we get to look a little bit more like Him, to act a little bit more like Him. That's the way it is with Jesus, going His way.

There are a lot of people around who claim to follow Jesus, but they are altogether too content with themselves, too complacent, too unthinking, and too satisfied that they're doing enough. They give very little evidence of having been with Jesus and of going His way. When one walks the way of Jesus, it's noticeable.

The way of Jesus is the only way. It is the way of repentance and faith, of forgiveness extended and accepted, of love, joy, and peace. It is a way marked by wonders with the power of God's

Holy Spirit behind it, in it, working through it. It takes total involvement, because Jesus' way is not to watch the fire without getting burned. Jesus is not a spectator, He is a participant and anyone going His way participates too.

Jesus went all the way. He stopped at nothing. What the world needs today are followers of Jesus who will go all the way with Him, stopping at nothing. In Jesus we can walk that way with a living, vibrant faith. "I am the way," He says, and there is no other.

13

He Is the Way to Be a Person

Have this mind among yourselves, which you have in Christ Jesus, who, though he was in the form of God, did not count equality with God a thing to be grasped, but emptied himself taking the form of a servant, being born in the likeness of men. And being found in human form he humbled himself and became obedient unto death, even death on a cross. (Phil. 2:5-8 RSV)

There was once a contest to find the shortest possible poem. The second-prize winner was an entry entitled "Fleas." It had two lines: "Adam had 'em." The first-prize winner was even shorter and it seemed to touch deeply into the real issue of life. Its title was "I." The poem consisted of one word: "Why?"

It's a question millions of people are asking these days: "Why I?" They want to know who they are. Philosophers and social scientists talk about today's identity crisis, and this is it. People feel cheapened by the kind of life they have to live. A man's labor is just a dispensable commodity to be purchased in the open market for the lowest price. A human being is a number on an identification tag, so that when he has been blown to bits his military record can be completed. A woman is just an object of lust, a "playmate." A competitor is just someone to be surpassed, no matter how. A home is just a place invaded by the endless radio and TV chatter of advertisers. Even the sacred days have been commercialized and cheapened to the point where for many people they have no meaning at all. Man has become a disfigured caricature of himself.

A lot of people look at themselves that way. They see themselves simply as the repository of the sex drive, the lust for power, and the brutal determination to survive at any cost. Having gone that way, and having given himself to that pursuit, a man wakes up one morning and asks himself some serious questions: "Why? Why am I? Why was I born? Why am I here? Where in the world am I going?"

Someone once declared that if you have one original idea a week, you are doing well. How many did you have this last week? How many did you have all last year? We do a lot of talking, and a little listening, but how much thinking do we do? Here is a thought: "Why?" Are you an IBM card or a man? Are you a housecleaner or a woman? Are you a name somewhere in a school file or are you a person with a past, present, and a future all your own? Are you worth something, or not? That's the question.

Are you an animal, maybe a higher form of animal, but still an animal? A lot of people think of themselves that way, and act accordingly. People who become animals are more savage than many of the other animals. Mere animals show some sense, but people who become mere animals show no sense at all.

It is recorded that Churchill once said, "The destiny of mankind is not decided by material computation. When great causes are on the move in the world . . . we learn that we are spirits, not animals, and that something is going on in space and time, and beyond space and time, which, whether we like it or not, spells duty." Or as one of those quotes in *Reader's Digest* has it, "We need not worry so much about what man descends from, it's what he descends *to* that shames the human race."

There has been a lot of talk about the dignity of man. Some of it sounds beautiful, but most of it is empty. Magnification of man looks pretty sick in the bright glare of what men are doing to themselves, and to each other. The world is not a pretty place, and men have made it so. If only someone would show us how to be men! If only someone would treat us as human beings, each with an identity of his own! If only someone would do that, maybe we could get out of this rat race, and be men again. If only someone would.

Someone has! In the gloom there is a light. It comes from a man on a very dark day hanging on a cross, outside a city wall. If we are looking for the way to be real men, real persons, He is the way. That is what He himself said, "I am the Way." It is about this one man that St. Paul was talking, having found from personal experience that He is the way. Of that one man, Paul said, "Have this mind among yourselves, which you have in Christ Jesus, who, though he was in the form of God, did not count equality with God a thing to be grasped, but emptied himself, taking the form of a servant being born in the likeness of men. And being found in human form, he humbled himself and became obedient unto death, even death on a cross" (Phil. 2:5-8 RSV).

If we talk about Jesus, we talk about man. If we look at Jesus, we see ourselves. In Jesus Christ it becomes clear that we are more than ingenious assemblies of portable plumbing. We are more than highly developed apes who have learned how to shave. We are persons, redeemed by the Son of the living God. He became a man to do that just for us. We are, as the Bible says, a little lower than the angels, a little less than God. Jesus Christ was made a little lower than the angels, for a little while giving up the full privilege of His deity, taking on himself our nature as human beings, becoming a man, a human person, like you and me to make us like Him.

We can go our own way, of course, if that's what we want to do. We are men, human persons, and we have that right. We probably have that disposition too. We don't even like to be told that we are not living up to our possibilities as men, as human persons. But there is Jesus, God's man, and we can't remove Him from the pages of history. We can ignore Him, and we can reject Him, but we can't destroy Him. He is there, God's man for all men, including us.

Jesus said, "I am the way. I am the way to be a man."

It's a great story, the story of that man. It begins quite simply in one Gospel: "This is the family record of Jesus Christ, who was a descendant of David, who was a descendant of Abraham" (Matt. 1:1 TEV). He was a man all right.

The same story begins quite differently in another Gospel, "Before the world was created, the Word already existed; he was with God, and he was the same as God. From the very beginning the Word was with God. God made the world through him, and yet the world did not know him. He came to his own country, but his own people did not receive him. Some, however, did receive him and believed in him; so he gave them the right to become God's children. They did not become God's children by natural means, by being born as the children of a human father; God himself was their Father. The Word became a human being and lived among us. We saw his glory, full of grace and truth. This was the glory which he received as the Father's only Son. . . . God gave the Law through Moses; but grace and truth came through Jesus Christ. No on has ever seen God. The only One, who is the same as God and is at the Father's side, has made him known" John 1:1-18 TEV).

St. John tells us that Jesus knew He came from God. He knew who He was. He was a man, not a rational beast. He was God's man, and also God's Son. He didn't have to be told what He was worth. He knew.

We are told that the most precious commodity in the world today is Californium-252, valued at $450 billion a pound. Would we say we're worth a pound of this rare element? Probably not to another human being, but to God we're worth a lot more. God sent His Son for us. God gave His only and eternal Son for us. That Son gave

His life on that dark day when our world did the worst to Him. Though He has the whole nature of God, He emptied himself of the privileges and prerogatives of His deity. He took human form and put himself in our place as a servant. He was obedient to His father because He was a dutiful Son. He was a man, and He had a mission. He was on His way, and nothing could stop Him. He didn't mind, if this is what it took to be Savior of the world. He didn't flinch at death. If this is where obedience would take Him, that is where He would go. For all of that, God has given Him a name which is above every other name, that at the name of Jesus every knee should bow in heaven and on earth and beneath the earth.

Hotel rooms often have a door knob hanger that can be placed on the outside of the door when one wants to sleep late. It says, "Do not disturb." It's the sign a lot of people have hung on the knobs of their lives. Let me alone, they say to God, and to everyone else, and I will let you alone. Let me enjoy myself and I'll let you enjoy yourself. Don't upset me, and I won't upset you. Don't make demands upon me, and I won't make demands upon you. Don't expect me to do anything, and I won't expect you to do anything. It has become almost a kind of religion with people that they want their privacy to be respected. They don't want to be disturbed.

The other side of that hotel sign often reads: "Maid service: Make up the room." Make it up, the sign says, while I'm out for breakfast, or out shopping or out conducting business. Make it up so that it's nice and comfortable when I come back. That is what a lot of people want the church to do for their own personal lives. They don't want to be involved, but the church is supposed to entertain them with fancy preaching. They want beautiful music and pleasant thoughts that will make them feel a little better while they involve themselves in other things, like eating breakfast, shopping, and making business calls.

Jesus was a real man. He didn't say, "Do not disturb me," and He didn't say, "Service please." This is what He said: "For the

Son of man is come to seek and to save that which was lost" (Luke 19:10). The Son of man came not to be served but to serve; He didn't have to do it, but He took upon himself the form of a servant, because He was a man.

I admit it isn't easy. His contemporaries despised Samaritans, and Jesus showed them kindness. The pillars of society exploited the poor, but Jesus said, "Happy are those who know they are spiritually poor: the kingdom of heaven belongs to them!" The people at that time thought of children as non-persons, but Jesus said, "Of such is the kingdom of heaven." Conformity was not His business. Neither was partiality. He was a man out for men, for every man, woman, and child. He knew who He was, and He wants each of us to know who we are. "I have redeemed you," He says to every man. To any man who will believe and follow He says "You are a man, and you are forgiven. Be a new man, renewed by the power of God through faith in me, and you are mine."

By faith in Jesus, we belong to a great people brought to life again. "Have faith in Me and come out of the darkness into the light, from the power of Satan to God, from the lostness which makes a man wonder who he is to the forgiveness which is foundness."

Jesus cares. He cares about us. He wants us to be real men, real persons. We are to be His men, with faith in Him, accepting His forgiveness, having His life. We are to know that we are real men with all the responsibilities and privileges of sons and daughters of God. "I am the way," says Jesus, "the way to be real men and women."

Jesus is man's friend, man's servant. He lived for us, and He died for us. Raised from the dead by the glory of His Father, *He lives*, He lives for us again. He has a name above every name. He can be trusted, and He can be followed. It takes a lot of trust, and some consecrated following. "I am the way," says Jesus. "I am the way for you to be genuine human beings."

"Jesus' men are gentlemen. There is nothing so moving as the tenderness of a gentleman. Jesus' women are ladies. There is nothing so fine as the warm-hearted love of a woman who knows Jesus and follows Him. There is nothing so sturdy and so attractive as the manliness of a boy who has made up his mind to go the way of Jesus. There is nothing more promising or more beautiful than the loveliness of a girl who has attached herself to Jesus and isn't afraid to be found in His company. People like that know who they are. They have found themselves, they have identity, they have a firm idea of where they are and where they're headed. They are on the way. "I am the way," says Jesus, "the way to be a real person."

Whoever we are, we count with Jesus. We don't have to protest or demonstrate to prove ourselves men, not with Jesus we don't. It doesn't make any difference with Jesus whether we have long hair or no hair. He is not impressed with our choice of clothes, either. He knows us. He wants us. He gave himself for us, and calls us to do the same for Him. That's the way to be real men, real persons.

14

He Is the Way to
Be a Friend

Jesus left that place, and as he walked along he saw a tax collector, named Matthew, sitting in his office. He said to him, "Follow me." Matthew got up and followed him. While Jesus was having dinner at his house, many tax collectors and outcasts came and joined him and his disciples at the table. Some Pharisees saw this and said to his disciples, "Why does your teacher eat with tax collectors and outcasts?" Jesus heard them and answered, "People who are well do not need a doctor, but only those who are sick. Go and find out what this scripture means, 'I do not want animal sacrifices, but kindness,' I have not come to call the respectable people, but the outcasts." (Matt. 9:9-13 TEV)

John Lennon of the Beatles was once reported to say, "Christianity will go. It will vanish and shrink. I needn't argue about that. I'm right, and I will be proved right. We [the Beatles] are more popular than Jesus Christ now. . . ."

The year was 1966, and it may have looked to some that the Beatles were more popular than Jesus Christ. But now John Lennon's confident prediction seems unlikely to come true. The Beatles are no longer a singing group, they have broken up and gone their separate ways. If this world of ours is still around a hundred years from now, I am positively certain that multitudes in many lands will know, honor, and love Jesus Christ. Mention the Beatles a hundred years from now, and maybe all the response one will get will be a mystified look.

What was it about Jesus Christ that fascinated people? We can look almost anywhere in the New Testament, and we will get an answer to that question. A look at the ninth chapter of Matthew quoted above, recounts in just a paragraph or two an incident and its sequel which are characteristic of Jesus.

Everyone needs friends, but where can we find them? Friendships are not easy to come by; they never were and now it's even tougher. Many people pay very little attention to one another. They don't care about one another, they don't know one another, and many don't even *want* to know anyone else very well. Friendship produces problems, and who needs more problems these days? Friendship creates responsibility, and who of us needs more responsibility? Friendship calls for a love of a high order, and who has love like that to give these days? Besides, everybody is on the move, and becoming friends with someone isn't worth it because it won't last anyway.

Friendship may have been important in the "good old days" when everybody lived in the same small town, went to the same church, attended the same high school, married the same kind of people, settled down on the family farm or became involved in the family business, and raised a number of children who duplicated the same process. Now things are different. Education, greater opportunities, a desire to improve, the lure of industrial centers, all these have combined to send families scurrying from one part of the country to another and even across national boundaries.

The young adult today is likely to have attended schools in two, three, four or more cities before graduation from high school. He may have gone to college in a different city, maybe a thousand miles away or even in another country. Military or some other voluntary service may send young men and women across the seas. In employment with a large corporation, one assignment may follow another before the family can settle itself more or less permanently in one community. Even then, they may have to move after a few years.

Even some older folks after retirement move to another place in the world because the climate is more congenial or for some other reason.

What I have described may sound like it is restricted to people only in the middle and upper income brackets. Actually, low income families do the same thing. They seek larger salaries or more productive work, and they move to get what they want. Migrant workers follow the farm crops. Young people roam around the country "finding themselves." Older sections of cities are torn down for urban renewal and hundreds of families are forced to relocate because they can't afford to live in the new buildings erected in the place of their old tenements.

Mobility is a fact of modern life, and it does things to human relationships. It keeps people from forming long and lasting friendships because they don't know where they will be next year. People hesitate to become too deeply involved, to commit themselves too much to neighbors and communities that surround them.

For the same reasons, the old-timers in an area isolate themselves from the newcomers who won't be there long enough anyway to understand the traditions and customs the old-timers have come to revere. As a result people get to know each other only on a superficial level. There are the people you meet in stores, the beauty parlor; the gas station attendant, the checker at the supermarket, the bus driver, the newspaper boy. Sometimes you know their first name, and more often you don't. It doesn't make much difference, they are just parts of the delivery system which satisfies some of our desires and needs. It isn't the best way to get to know people, and it may not be even very good business, but that's the way it is.

Then there are other people whom we get to know at club meetings, Rotary, PTA, or at church. Neighbors and fellow employees might seem to be better candidates for genuine friendship. They see each other regularly, have certain common interests, appear to be working toward similar goals. Even in a middle-sized business, however, it is not unusual for an executive to know only the names and very little else about the people in his own department. The same executive has little more than nodding acquaintance with the husbands of the women with whom his wife has coffee at least once a week and the fathers of the children who play with his own children every day. He doesn't know them, and the fact is, he really doesn't care to. Then there are the relatives. Uncle Charlie hasn't been seen in ten years, and Cousin Mary died last month. After a while, Christmas letters (mimeographed) are filled with names vaguely remembered.

It isn't unusual these days to find families, even brothers and sisters who don't have very deep feelings for one another. They treat each other more like casual acquaintances than as children of the same parents who grew up together in the same family.

What is it like to have a real friend, a close friend, someone you can trust, in whom you can confide? A lot of people don't have anyone like that at all. They themselves couldn't be friends like that to anyone else either. They haven't any real bonds with anyone.

Anyway, what is it that makes a friend? Well, there is something about him or her that is special. What is it about friends? It isn't so much what they *do* as what they *are*. What *are* they, anyway? They are genuinely interested, that's what. They care. They have something inside of them that reaches out and touches you. They don't care whether you are rich or poor, whether you are as educated as they are or not, whether you are famous or unknown. They just care, that's all. They care about you. That's a friend.

It's one thing that made Jesus the man He was. "You are my

friends," He said, and there has never been quite another like Him. "Greater love has no man than this," He said, "that a man lay down his life for his friends" (John 15:13 RSV). When He said that, He was talking about himself.

Jesus went where the action was. He took the initiative. He didn't barricade himself off somewhere, waiting for people to bring their troubles to Him. He was always out there with the people. He was with them on the road, in their homes, on their jobs, a friend reaching out because He cared.

He was there, on a cross, reaching out to the whole world as a friend. As St. Paul put it: "While we were yet sinners Christ died for us" (Rom. 5:8 RSV). I have never been able to understand how some people can pass that by, as if it never happened, or as if it doesn't mean anything to them. Yet people do pass it by, all the time, and there are more of them now, perhaps, than ever before. It is the way of our world. We just don't care. We don't care about God, and we don't care about one another. The two seem to go together.

Jesus cared. He met all kinds of people, and He cared about them all. He put some people to the test of friendship, but He never turned anyone away. "Him that cometh to me," He said, "I will in no wise cast out" (John 6:37).

The life of Jesus was a constant caring, and the dying of Jesus is the ultimate evidence that He cared. He cared enough for all of us to give His innocent life for our sins. He did it for us, not for himself. He *is* a friend. His Father recognized that tremendous obedience of His, that magnificent caring, by raising Him from the dead and giving Him a name that is above every other name. His name is Jesus. He is the Savior of the world, and He is our friend, yours and mine.

Jesus said, "I am the way." He is the way to forgiveness and life. He is the way to friendship with God and to friendship with our fellowmen. He not only shows the way, but He is the way. In Jesus, with faith in Him, with confident reliance upon Him, all of us can learn again how to be friends and how to make friends with people around us. We don't have to be afraid of that. With Jesus, we can have the courage of friendship.

There is one remarkable thing I have observed about Jesus. He was a good listener. His very presence invited people around Him to open up. He was sympathetic, understanding, fair, honest, and kind. Give Him a problem, and He went right to the heart of it. When some friends brought Him a man who had been a paralytic all his life, Jesus said to the stricken man: "Your sins are forgiven you." It sounds irrelevant to our secular age, I know, but it is the most relevant thing God can ever say to a man. He says it to me and to you. He goes right to the heart of the problem. He cares about us.

Jesus didn't hesitate to meet the people who needed Him most. He didn't confine His ministry to the "nice" people of His day, to the upper middle class, let's say, to the people who knew how to say and do all the right things. The fact is, He had the most disturbing assortment of friends. There were some unlearned fishermen, prostitutes, a tax collector, and various other characters who had fallen afoul of the law, plus some other undesirables. Yes, there were some from the upper and middle classes too. But He sought out the outcasts, the ones who didn't have a friend in the world. He was a friend, and there never has been anyone else like Him.

Not everyone whose life He touched became His friend. That did not stop Him. He was and is willing to accept all kinds of people. For Him there are no untouchables. His love is for all. The Good News of Jesus is for all. He offers His friendship to all.

No one can be so bad that Jesus will deny him forgiveness. "Can you every forgive me?" says a husband confessing to his wife an affair with someone else. "I love you," she says, even though she is deeply hurt. Her love covers the hurt and also the sin. It is like that love of Jesus. "[The] love [of Christ] covers a multitude of sins" (1 Pet. 4:8 RSV).

Jesus was abused, scorned, stepped on, spit on, but He kept on coming. Nothing could stop Him. He cared and He cares. That is the Good News of Jesus. It is not the Good News of our world, because none of us is made that way. We have to be *remade* by the love of Jesus. We learn from Him how to go that way. It takes a lot of effort. But He did it. He died for us, and *He lives* for us. He calls to us, "I am the way. I am the way to true and lasting friendship." "Those who hear my words and follow my commandments," Jesus says, "these are the people who really are my friends."

If Jesus is the way, most of us had better look to our priorities. Time is short, and there is no better time than now to change our way of doing things. Jesus spoke softly, and left the big stick at home. He didn't go around boasting about himself and loudly proclaiming how good He was. "Good Master," someone addressed Him one day. Jesus replied, "Why do you call me good?" He was a friend, and He did not hesitate to make friends.

He was always out there with the people. As he left one place and walked along to the next, He saw a tax collector named Matthew sitting at his toll booth. Jesus said to him, "Follow me." We don't know what else passed between them, whether it was a smile, a word, or what, but He just said, "Follow me," and Matthew got up and followed Him. A short time afterward, He was sitting at Matthew's house having dinner. Matthew invited in his friends. It was a strange collection, but they were his friends. There were many tax collectors and outcasts who came and joined Jesus and His disciples at the table. Some decent church people saw this and said to His disciples, "Why does your teacher eat with tax collectors and outcasts?" Jesus heard them and answered, "People who are well do not need a doctor, but only those who are sick. Go and find out what this scripture means. 'I do not want animal sacrifices, but kindness.' I have not come to call the respectable people, but the outcasts."

Whenever you do something positive, something helpful, you can expect some criticism. Very often that criticism comes from the strangest quarters, from people who ought to know better.

They feel themselves challenged and so they defend themselves by criticizing others. It could be that we have done the very same thing ourselves.

We have to remember that heaven is going to be the abode not of the good, but of redeemed. Jesus came not to reassure the healthy but to heal the sick; not to congratulate the righteous but to call sinners to repentance. There is joy in heaven over one sinner who repents, rather than over the smugness and self-congratulation, mingled with suspicion of others, that characterizes many who think of themselves as righteous and religious.

"I am the way," says Jesus. He invites His friends to follow that way. It is a vocation to spontaneous joyful fellowship. His is the call to enjoy the earth rather than to plunder and pollute it, to enjoy other people rather than use them, to enjoy ourselves rather than be forever nervously upholding our "image."

With faith in Jesus, enjoy life. With confidence in Him, open the doors of friendship. As friends of Jesus, let us make friends with others. Receive Jesus as the friend He is, taking His forgiveness as our own, making His life our life. Jesus is our friend. Let's learn from Him how to be a friend, how to make friends. Let's forget ourselves, as He forgot himself, and learn to care, as He cares. He says, "I am the way. I am the way to friendship, freely extended with no strings attached." Let's go His way for it is the only way.

15

He Is the Way to Overcome

Let us give thanks to the God and Father of our Lord Jesus Christ, the merciful Father, the God from whom all help comes! He helps us in all our troubles, so that we are able to help those who have all kinds of troubles, using the same help that we ourselves have received from God. Just as we have a share in Christ's many sufferings, so also through Christ we share in his great help. If we suffer, it is for your help and salvation; if we are helped, then you too are helped and given the strength to endure with patience the same sufferings that we also endure. So our hope in you is never shaken; we know that just as you share in our sufferings, you also share in the help we receive. (2 Cor. 1:3-7 TEV)

Discouragement is something like the common cold; almost everybody gets it once in a while. Some of us get it a lot, and some of us are all but overcome by it. St. Paul must have realized this fact. After his normal greetings to the people at Corinth at the beginning of his second letter to them, he went on to say the beautiful words quoted above.

Discouragement is easy to come by and hard to get rid of. It is like a poison that does its work deep down inside. It saps a man's strength and destroys his spirit. It makes even strong men do things, say things, and think things which surprise even themselves. Deep-rooted ills can often be pinpointed, brought out into the open, and solutions found for them because they are now identified. Discouragement is tougher. It often acts like a general malaise, a sick feeling all over. It isn't enough to say to the discouraged, "Get with it and get over it."

There is a story told about a man who went to see his doctor because he was feeling bad all over. The doctor recognized that it was more a thing of spirit than a physical ailment. "I have just the answer for you," the doctor said. "Go to the circus in town this week and let that superbly funny clown cheer you up."

"That won't work doctor," the man said dejectedly, "I am that clown."

Maybe at times we're that clown. Maybe we're the life of the party, cheering other people up. We could be the head of an enterprise involved in helping others solve their problems. We could be the head of a household, keeping the family's head above water and meeting family problems with the courage and insight expected of us. All the while, deep down inside, we feel depressed ourselves.

We shouldn't be surprised for there are many others like us. It is human to have ambitions and human to be disappointed. It's human to be lifted up by the bright days, and to be cast down on the dark days. It's human to try, and it's also human to get tired of trying when it doesn't seem to work. It's human to laugh, and it's human to cry. We have a lot of company.

As Job said, "Although affliction cometh not forth of the dust, neither doth trouble spring out of the ground; yet man is born unto trouble, as the sparks fly upward (Job 5:6,7). Trouble is the unwelcome guest at some time or other in every life. Trouble has a partner who always comes along. Trouble comes and goes, but the partner whose name is discouragement takes up residence and tries to make himself comfortable. If we let discouragement take over, it becomes a worse trouble.

A minister once asked some of the members of his church what caused them to become discouraged. Some said it was the church itself. Others said it was the excuses people gave for not helping when it was needed. Others said it was the people who always insist on criticizing but never stop to look at themselves. Still others were discouraged by personal problems, financial obligations and the constant rise in the cost of living, and the fact that hard work, initiative, and honesty are not appreciated.

Some of the young people commented on the sources of their discouragement. One said, "I am discouraged because my parents always complain." Another said, "What discourages me is one of my teachers. She gives so much homework that I've no time for any other subjects." Another said, "I get discouraged when I flunk a test even though I studied hard for it." A boy got discouraged because, as hard as he played, his team still lost the football game.

Young people are discouraged by their studies, and older people are often discouraged by the actions and attitudes of the young. There are young women who are discouraged because they are unable to find suitable mates who will live up to their expectations. Old and young alike are discouraged by wars and threats of wars, violence in our streets, racial and national prejudice, pollution and starvation. In spite of all the intelligence, affluence, and resources which could be brought to bear on these problems, they just don't think anything will work and they are discouraged.

We might say that discouragement is the illness of our age. We don't have to be members of any particular church to be discouraged; just being members of a church is not the answer to discouragement. It is there, eating into the vitals of life, and nothing seems to help, nothing works.

In the first century of our calendar there was a man who stood up to say "Have faith." He was not talking about some faith or other that might or might not put a different light on the situation. When he talked about faith, it was always faith in Jesus Christ. He himself had met Jesus, personally. From that time on, everything was different for him. He knew Jesus was crucified, but he knew that Jesus was alive. He heard the call of the living Jesus, "Get up on your feet and go," and he followed it. That's what faith is: following Christ, trusting Him, and going His way. A man named Saul found that way; following it in faith he became Paul.

Paul says, "Let us give thanks to the God and Father of our Lord Jesus Christ, the merciful Father, the God from whom all help comes! He helps us in all our troubles, so that we are able to help those who have all kinds of troubles, using the same help that we ourselves have received from God" (2 Cor. 1:3,4 TEV).

I wish I could tell you, Paul said, that I never had any troubles. I wish I could tell you that you won't have any troubles. I can't tell you that. I have troubles, lots of them, and I know you do too. No matter what the trouble is, he went on to say, I don't allow myself the luxury of getting discouraged. There isn't time enough for it and there really isn't room for it. I have only one reason for saying this, "*Christ lives* and God has proved himself to be a Father. That makes everything different. He turns the world upside down, and He has turned me inside out."

"We know what it means to fear the Lord, and so we try to persuade men. God knows us completely, and I hope that in your hearts you know me as well. Are we really insane? It is for God's sake. Or are we sane? It is for your sake. We are ruled by Christ's love for us, now that we recognize that one man died for all men, which means that all men take part in his death. He died for all men so that those who live should no longer live for themselves, but only for him who died and was raised to life for their sake" (2 Cor. 5:11-15 TEV). That's the way Paul talked. When discouragement came to him as it does to all men, faith in Jesus burned it away as the sun burns up the mist on a foggy morning.

"When anyone is joined to Christ he is a new being; the old is gone, the new has come. All this is done by God who through

Christ changed us from enemies into his friends, and gave us the task of making others his friends also. Our message is that God was making friends of all men through Christ. God did not keep an account of their sins against them, and he has given us the message of how he makes them his friends" (2 Cor. 5:17-19 TEV). Now Paul was a man who found out for himself whom to believe. If we don't know whom we believe, maybe we don't believe anybody. We have been misled many times and now we say, "I've had it! I don't believe anybody." In a way, we can't be blamed; that's the way discouragement talks, and we must be discouraged.

Now let's listen to this: "Here we are, then, speaking for Christ, as though God himself were appealing to you through us: on Christ's behalf, we beg you, let God change you from enemies into friends! Christ was without sin, but for our sake God made him share our sin in order that we, in union with him, might share the righteousness of God" (2 Cor. 5:20,21 TEV). That's the gospel, the Good News of Jesus, and it is verified by His life, guaranteed by His death. A man who is out to mislead you doesn't lay his life on the line for you as He did. He said, "I am the way," and He meant it.

Jesus proved it once and for all. He went all the way, not in honor but in dishonor, not to the plaudits of the crowd but in circumstances that would justify almost any kind of discouragement. Nobody could blame Him for being discouraged, but He wasn't. Like the man He was, He leveled with His Father, "My God, my God, why have you abandoned me?" Like the Son of God He was, He emerged triumphant. "It is finished. My Father, into your hands I hand over my spirit."

We can believe Him, we really can. No matter what has happened to us, we can believe Him. We can go with Him all the way. If we follow Him, we will not be brought all the way down by discouragement. I can promise you that because He said "I am the way," and He means it.

Jesus Christ is alive. Since that's true, it is possible to live by faith in Him without all of the discouragement which would ordinarily settle on all of our lives. Despite all the trouble that comes our way it is possible to live with that exuberant spirit which gives thanks to God and the Father of our Lord Jesus Christ, the merciful Father, the God from whom all help comes. He helps us in all our troubles, using the same help that we ourselves have received from God. Just as we have a share in Christ's many sufferings, so also through Christ we share in His great help as He promises life to everyone who follows Him. The follower of Jesus, like Jesus himself, just wades right through the discouragement. He rides right over it. He overcomes.

God has His own way of turning trouble into triumph. He does that through the faith He gives. I have seen it in people, people who had trouble but who nevertheless helped me, through their faith in Jesus. Maybe they had their trouble in order to help me. That is the way God does things. It's the way He did them in Jesus, the way He does them in people today who follow Jesus.

St. Paul, who had known a lot of suffering in his lifetime, said, "If we suffer, it is for your help and salvation; if we are helped, then you too are helped and given the strength to endure with patience the same sufferings that we also endure. So our hope in you is never shaken; we know that just as you share in our sufferings, you also share in the help we receive" (2 Cor. 1:6,7 TEV).

There is community in trouble, and there is community in help as well. We are all in the same boat, we all have troubles. There is also a community of help. Jesus died for all of us, and *Jesus lives* to give His life to all. The offer comes to all of us, and it comes from Jesus himself. "I am come that you might have life, and have it in abundance." We can have life by faith in Jesus; have faith in Him and overcome. *He lives*. We can live with Him, courageously, joyfully, victoriously.

Are we discouraged with ourselves? Jesus is the way to overcome! He forgives all the wrongs, the hurts, the offenses, the sins, that have caused the breaks in our lives. In forgiveness He stretches out His hands to us and He accepts us. We are to accept ourselves in Him, always in Him.

Are we discouraged about the way others treat us? They are probably just as discouraged as we are, and they show it. Whose hand is going to be held out to them in forgiveness, if it isn't ours? Who is going to help them, if we don't? Jesus helps us in our troubles, so that we may be able to help others using the same help that we ourselves have received from God in Jesus Christ.

That's the way we follow Him. It is the way of Jesus. We have a share in His suffering and we share His great help. We share it with those whom we know and those whom we don't know. We help as we are helped. That is the way of Jesus. That is what the church is to be, a community of help for a world that needs help very much.

When we trust Jesus and go with Him all the way, disappointment becomes just a sieve where the little things go through and the big things remain. The big things are faith, hope, love, courage in trouble, and kindness to those who know trouble. It is the witness of one with conviction of the truth of God in Jesus, that He is really God and He really helps. Jesus says, "I am the way." He means it! He is the only way.

16

He Is the Way to Cope with Today

All things are done according to God's plan and decision; and God chose us to be his own people in union with Christ because of his own purpose, based on what he had decided from the very beginning. (Eph. 1:11 TEV)

Jesus is the way to cope with the chaos of our world today. St. Paul declared that to his time and to his world which was faced with chaos and disorder and for which there seemed to be no solution. He declared it with the words quoted above.

If that is true, it puts a new face on the whole business. God has a purpose, a kind of secret purpose for the whole world. The secret is disclosed for the first time in His Son, Jesus Christ. Something great has happened which we can ignore at the risk of opening ourselves to more chaos. There is an order established in this universe of ours, and it's going to come out in the open even more than it has already. "In all his wisdom and insight God did what he had purposed, and made known to us the secret plan he had already decided to complete by means of Christ. God's plan, which he will complete when the time is right, is to bring all creation together, everything in heaven and on earth, with Christ as head. All things are done according to God's plan and decision" (Eph. 1:8-11 TEV).

What St. Paul says is that God has a plan. Jesus is the key to that plan. With Him things began, and with Him things get pulled together again.

Talk like that doesn't exactly ring a bell with many people these days. They see chaos all around, and they are very much impressed with it. They see problems for which there seem to be no solutions. They find no answer to the youth revolution, the sexual revolution, the political revolution, the economic disasters, and to what some call the religious revolution.

People are troubled and they are disturbed. Even more than that, they are frantic, unable to think clearly and so they give vent to violent emotions. What is more, they don't see themselves as frantic or despairing. They think they are reacting quite naturally to a problem which can only be described as chaos, where man has nowhere to turn and no way to get out.

If the various revolutions moved in a straight line, something might be done about them. The trouble is that they move backwards and forward, sideways, and in several directions. One day something looks good, and the next day it looks bad. How can we get hold of something like that? How can we find our way through it?

Chaos can move in and take hold very quickly. Our world and our lives are beset before and behind with all kinds of pressures and demands that have to be satisfied, while the normal problems of life and death crowd in upon us. Today we are all living on the edge of a volcano; the steam is rising and the whole thing threatens to blow off. We have felt the heat and seen the sparks of our time and age. It could be that we have not yet faced the hot burning lava that is to come. How do we stand up to all that stuff, the stuff that produces disorder and constitutes chaos, the stuff that seems almost too hot to handle?

Millions of people today just run away. They live in a dream world, wishing to return to the past. The past looks very attractive to them, and they prefer to sleepwalk through the present in the hope that the future may turn out to be as quiet as they imagine the past to have been. All of us are tempted to do this. We try to cope with chaos by avoiding it, acting as if it doesn't exist. We talk about it as a passing fad that will change one of these days, and then we'll wake up to a new world where everything will be right again. Riots will go away, sex will no longer be the center of movies and entertainment, LSD will just be a memory, and decent clothing styles will come back. One day, we say, the good times will return.

Well, I'm sorry but I have to declare that the past is dead and gone. It will never return. All that lives from the past is the guilt that we inherit from it. It haunts us and it helps to make the present chaos even more unlivable. People are still what they were, selfish and sinful, too busy to be concerned about others, too intent in getting ahead to be bothered helping anyone else, too hopeful of finding the secret of life in self-satisfaction, too self-centered to be truly human, too ready to go their own way instead of God's way. Now that's sin. It has always been sin, it is sin today and will be sin tommorow.

The remarkable thing is that people still go on dreaming that they can cope with chaos on their own. Man refuses to see how frail he really is, how incapable of fighting his own way out of the chaos which he himself has helped to create. There are no pat answers to that chaos. The issues are complex and profound, the questions growing in number. What happens? People become so absorbed in themselves, in their pain, in their anguish that they make their own hell. Hell is man turned in upon himself with only himself to turn to: no God, no need of forgiveness, no expectation of real hope, no real life—nothing but chaos.

Things are not going to get any better. We don't need to be told that the world population is growing by leaps and bounds. For years we've struggled with the causes of disease, in order to prolong life. But the problem seems to be that the older are living longer and there's not enough room for all of us. So the world

107

comes up with a practical and simple solution: the legal wholesale butchery of the unborn through abortion. This really doesn't solve the problem, it just continues the process of our being dehumanized.

The proponents of population control tell us that this must be done because experiments with rats proved that normal rats become belligerent, destructive and vicious when large numbers are crowded into a limited space. So there it is—humans are simply rats of a higher order.

The problem of human hostility and aggressiveness has always been with us. More people only make it more visible, more pronounced, and more destructive. Cutting down on the population won't change it, because it will still be there. It was there when Cain killed Abel, and it's with us today. We see it everywhere, in large cities and in rural areas, in depressed areas and affluent suburbs, in communities and even in churches. Wherever there are people, there are the ingredients that produce chaos with which people are trying to cope, all on their own, without any real change in themselves and no hope of change in the world around them.

The Washington National Institute of Mental Health drew these conclusions about human society from their experiments: "The frustrations of urban society are forcing on each citizen knowledge of his own nature; that we never have been and never shall be created equal; that we get along more because we must rather than because we want to; that we are aggressive beings easily given to violence."

We really didn't need the psychologists to tell us that. The Bible has been saying that for a long time. Out of the heart of man proceed violent thoughts. These thoughts are easily converted into violent actions. The thoughts themselves tell us what man is and the actions that proceed from these thoughts show us what he is. Man is at the bottom of the chaos in the world today. There is no hope in coping with chaos which avoids the problem itself, and that problem is man.

We are the real problem. Multiply our willfulness, our selfishness, our lovelessness, our unconcern and indifference by more than four billion, and we see what is at the bottom of the chaos in the world.

Is there no way of coping with chaos? The Bible never blinked at the problem. It doesn't give us twelve easy steps to successful living. It gives us only one way. The Bible keeps talking about Jesus, the one extraordinary man in all of human history. He was a man by the design of God who has a plan for this world of ours. God knows all about chaos, and that's why Jesus came. In the fulness of His manhood, He put the whole power of His divine sonship with the Father to work for His fellowmen of every age and nation. In His thinking no lines were drawn, and in His acting no boundaries set. It isn't as if He died for just some good people and not for all others. He found us all in the same boat, in the midst of chaos, and He died for us all.

Many times in my charismatically-renewed ministry I have invited people to accept Jesus Christ as their Savior, to join His company of the redeemed, to anchor their lives to Him by faith. Some of them have told me boldly, "I don't know why it's necessary. I have never done anything that I'm really *that* ashamed of." More than anything else, this probably illustrates the problem of our world. People just don't see themselves as they are. They *won't* see themselves as they are. They have to build a little fence around themselves, to hold off all those watchful eyes that might see them as they are. Our world spends a lot of its energy holding God off at arm's length, trying to keep Him from interfering, avoiding even the mention of His name. The only time some people mention God at all is to curse somebody else. Meanwhile, the chaos grows apace, becoming mountainous in size, impenetrable in density, and absolutely destructive in its effects.

Through it all, through the chaos, shines the light of God. We can hear His voice. He speaks to our world, in the midst of chaos, with His ultimate word. God's word is in His Son Jesus Christ. It is a word of freedom. By the death of Jesus we are set free, and our sins are forgiven. In all of His wisdom and insight God did what He purposed. He made known to us the secret plan which He had already decided to complete by means of Jesus. God's plan, which He will bring to final completion when the time is right is to bring all creation together, everything in heaven and earth, with Christ as head. For all things are done according to God's plan and decision. God chose us to be His own people in union with Jesus because of His own purpose, based on what He had decided from the very beginning.

That's what the Bible says. That's the way the Bible talks to everyone who has come to know Jesus as Savior. Some accept it, and others do not. That is the tragedy of our world and that's the reason for the chaos.

It is still the glory of the grace of God that Jesus commands faith. He commands obedience, love and the courage to go with Him as His man or woman. With Jesus, chaos clears and eternity comes into view. With that view the world gets a different look. With God in command, as He is in Jesus, all of life comes to look different. God has a plan, to redeem this world of ours. That plan is in operation right now. Jesus died once, and it won't happen again. All who put their trust in Jesus are set free, their sins forgiven. This is the greatness of God's grace and the magnificence of His plan!

Jesus is the key to redemption and the key to completion. He died and rose again. He is Lord and no one is ever going to take that from Him. God loves this world of ours. Love is behind His purpose. He doesn't want anyone to be lost but that everyone should turn from His sin and be saved by His grace through faith in Jesus.

Jesus is the way to cope with today. He is the center for new life. When He becomes a reality in our lives, we will discover what St. Paul was talking about. God has indeed chosen us to be His own men and women in Jesus because of His own purpose, based on what He decided from the very beginning. What is more, it also becomes clear in Jesus that God has a plan and everything happens according to His plan and decision. Things can look bad today, but tomorrow they will be different, not because we make it so, but because all things are done according to God's plan and decision.

If that's true, there's only one thing to do. Open up to God. We can't hide from Him. Open up to God and His forgiveness in Jesus. We need that forgiveness. Open up to God and the new life in Jesus. We need that life. Open up to God and to the obedience of faith in Jesus. We need to know Him, to follow Him, to obey Him. Open up to the grace of God in Jesus and we'll receive that hope without which life cannot make sense. "I am the way," Jesus says, "the way to cope with chaos and confusion, today."

PART III

JESUS AND HIS CHURCH

17

The Shepherd and His Sheep

"I am the good shepherd. The good shepherd is willing to die for the sheep. The hired man, who is not a shepherd and does not own the sheep, leaves them and runs away when he sees a wolf coming; so the wolf snatches the sheep and scatters them. The hired man runs away because he is only a hired man and does not care for the sheep. I am the good shepherd. As the Father knows me and I know the Father, in the same way I know my sheep and they know me. And I am willing to die for them. There are other sheep that belong to me that are not in this sheepfold. I must bring them too; they will listen to my voice, and they will become one flock with one shepherd. The Father loves me because I am willing to give up my life, in order that I may receive it back again. No one takes my life away from me. I give it up of my own free will. I have the right to give it, and I have the right to take it back. This is what my Father has commanded me to do." Again there was a division among the Jews because of these words. Many of them were saying, "He has a demon! He is crazy! Why do you listen to him?' But others were saying, "A man with a demon could not talk like this! How could a demon open the eyes of a blind man?" The time came to celebrate the Feast of Dedication in Jerusalem; it was winter.

Jesus was walking around in Solomon's porch in the temple, when the Jews gathered around him and said, "How long are you going to keep us in suspense? Tell us the plain truth: are you the Messiah?" Jesus answered, "I have already told you, but you would not believe me. The works I do by my Father's authority speak on my behalf; but you will not believe because you are not my sheep. My sheep listen to my voice; I know them, and they follow me. I give them eternal life, and they shall never die; and no one can snatch them away from me. What my Father has given me is greater than all, and no one can snatch them away from the Father's care. The Father and I are one." (John 10:11-30 TEV)

When Jesus said, "I am the good shepherd," He didn't have to draw a picture for the people of His time. They knew what He was talking about because they were familiar with shepherds and their way of life. Most of us today have lived in cities and the only sheep we know about wind up as lamb chops at our dinner tables. As for shepherds, we have a little trouble identifying with what is now a dying breed of hardy people.

But Jesus was not explaining shepherds. He was explaining himself:

I am the good shepherd. The good shepherd is willing to die for the sheep. The hired man, who is not a shepherd and does not own the sheep, leaves them and runs away when he sees a wolf coming; so the wolf snatches the sheep and scatters them. The hired man runs away because he is only a hired man and does not care for the sheep. I am the good shepherd. As the Father knows me and I know the Father, in the same way I know my sheep and they know me. And I am willing to die for them. There are other sheep that belong to me that are not in this sheepfold. I must bring them, too; they will listen to my voice, and they will become one flock with one shepherd.

The oneness of the whole arrangement is the impressive thing.

In a world torn apart by its hatreds and hostilities, its envy and its selfishness, there is this shepherd and there is his flock. The two belong together and cannot be separated. The shepherd and His flock are Jesus and His church. That is one thing a lot of us tend to forget. Enemies of the church down through the ages wouldn't believe it. Their bones are rotting in the sands of time, but the church lives. Even some people inside the church act as if it isn't true. One would almost think the whole thing depends on them. No matter how impressive these people may be, there is only one who can talk justifiably like that, and He says, "My sheep will listen to my voice and there will be one flock and one shepherd."

When we think of it, most of us do not like to be compared to sheep because, even though sheep are likable, they can be very dumb, erratic, and helpless without leadership. They do such stupid things because their little brains can't figure how to keep them out of trouble. Isn't it ironic that human history is largely a story of people defeating the causes they thought were advancing? Dictators have come upon the scene promising restoration of law and order, and their rules have become the bloodiest tyrannies of all time. If we want to make comparisons, the sheep don't come off badly at all.

The comparison goes back a long way. Isaiah said, "All we like sheep have gone astray; we have turned every one to his own way" (Isa. 53:6 RSV). The diagnosis is simple, direct, swift, and devastating. That is the way it is. A person with everything to live for throws it away for frivolity. Successful businessmen proceed to make messes of their lives with utterly unbelievable and brainless performances in the area of personal relationships. A young man with his whole future before him won't listen to anybody. He has to have his own way, even if it means wrecking his life. It's the human story: "All we like sheep have gone astray, we have turned everyone to his own way."

St. Matthew tells us that Jesus looked upon the crowds and felt compassion. They were like sheep milling about without a shepherd. "I am the good shepherd . . . willing to die for the sheep." There are plenty of hired men around, but only one shepherd. The hired men are willing to lead, up to a point, but only the shepherd is willing to bleed for the sheep.

Jesus did not treat the waywardness of man lightly. He didn't pass off the problem of humanity as we often do, half jokingly and half wistfully when we say, "To err is human." Of course it is human, but that is not the end of it. Jesus, the Son of God, came into our world to live and to die as proof of the desperate situation of man, tangled in his sin, his mistakes, his malice. Jesus could not afford the luxury of maudlin sentimentality which assumes that the situation of man is not as bad as the preachers make it out to be. Jesus said man is not what he was meant to be and left on his own he will never be. The situation will not get better, it will only get worse. People are like sheep who can't find their own way. He said, "I am the good shepherd . . . willing to die for the sheep."

Sacrifice is the heart of salvation. Most parents sacrifice, give up things for their children, and that's great. They do it because they love. Nothing else could make them do it. But we always hear from parents who complain that their sacrifices have been received only with ingratitude. It seems that they want something in return for their sacrifices; to gain, not to lose. Love without thought of return is the love of Jesus and it makes Him unique. He is the one shepherd our world needs, for without Him the lostness of our world cannot be overcome. St. Paul said that the love of Jesus is almost beyond belief; it is beyond the limitations of human knowledge. Jesus was aware of that; what He felt inside reminded Him of His Father: "The Father loves me because I am willing to give up my life, in order that I may receive it back again. No one takes my life away from me. I give it up of my own free will. I have the right to give it, and I have the right to take it back. This is what my Father has commanded me to do." The shepherd pleads and leads; He is Jesus Christ, Son of God and Savior of the world.

Jesus died. That is a historical fact. He died for the sins of the world. That is the faith of the church. In the world there are more and more people who have faith that Jesus died for all, including them. This is the kind of faith that says: "Jesus died for all and He died for me." We can say that right now and right now it will be true for us. We don't have to know everything about Jesus to say it. We know He died for all, and that includes us.

Right now all we have to do is to turn from our own way and say to Jesus, "I believe you. You died for me." We can say that to Him directly because He is alive. Jesus gave His life willingly. He sacrificed himself out of pure love. He died for us, and received His life back again. He was raised from the dead by the glory of His Father. *He lives*. He is alive. He is Lord and He commands our faith. We shouldn't be afraid to say it to Him. "I believe you." In that act of faith there is forgiveness for the past and life for the future.

Nothing but faith will do, faith in Jesus the living Lord. It isn't easy. I know. It wasn't easy for the people who walked with Him before He died; they saw His miracles but kept on asking, "How long are you going to keep us in suspense? Tell us the plain truth: Are you the Messiah?" Jesus answered: "I have already told you, but you would not believe me. The works I do by my Father's authority speak on my behalf; but you will not believe because you are not my sheep. My sheep listen to my voice; I know them, and they follow me. I give them eternal life, and they shall never die; and no one can snatch them away from me. What my Father has given me is greater than all, and no one can snatch them away from the Father's care. The Father and I are one. " This is a plain statement of fact.

The oneness of it all is singularly impressive. Look at Jesus, and we see God. Anybody who knows Jesus, follows Him. That is the one thing in this world of ours that makes sense: to follow Him. The people who believe in Jesus and follow Him are His church.

When Jesus looked at the people in front of Him, all of them of one nationality, one country, one family, He said: "There are

119

other sheep that belong to me that are not in this sheepfold. I must bring them, too; they will listen to my voice, and they will become one flock with one shepherd." That is the way it is. There is one body, and Jesus is the head. There is one flock, and He is the shepherd. You can't split up Jesus and His Father, and you can't split up Jesus and His church. It is all one, one in Him.

There are all kinds of people in His church, all kinds of sheep in His flock. Some bear scars, and some don't. Some have had a rough time, and some have known peace all their lives. Some have had great experiences of faith, arriving at their convictions in a dramatic way. Others with faith just as deep never had such an experience. It isn't the experience that saves, but faith in Jesus Christ. "My sheep listen to my voice; I know them, and they follow me. I give them eternal life, and they shall never suffer eternal death; and no one can snatch them from me."

There are all kinds of folds in this flock of His. There isn't one congregation of Christians exactly like another one. Each one is made up of different people. It is an illusion to think that the one church of Jesus is going to look exactly the same all over the world. It just doesn't and never will. The church is the army of the living God made up of many regiments, each with a character of its own.

There is really only one unifying element in the life of the church throughout the world. Jesus Christ is its head. There is only one flock and only one shepherd. There may be many folds, but only one flock. Wherever Jesus Christ is head, there is His church.

Some flock together to follow the shepherd. There are some people around called pastors, which is another name for shepherds. They are not hired hands, they speak for Jesus. They want people to hear His voice and follow Him; not to follow them, but to follow Him. You can always tell the difference between a true shepherd and a hired hand. The hired hand thinks of himself, but the shepherd thinks of the sheep. The true shepherd hears the voice of Jesus, and follows Him so that the people whom he serves will follow Jesus because they hear Jesus' voice speaking through their shepherd.

The people of Jesus know Him. They hear His voice and follow Him. It is the way of their salvation for He is the shepherd. He is the way.

18

The Fellowship of Worship

But the time is coming, and is already here, when the real worshipers will worship the Father in spirit and in truth. These are the worshipers the Father wants to worship him. God is Spirit, and those who worship him must worship in spirit and in truth. (John 4:23,24 TEV)

Some people think that there is no place in the modern world for worship. "We have gone beyond all of that ancient superstition," some say. The dedicated atheists of the Communist world make a big deal of their supposedly scientific efforts to kill the idea of God and destroy every vestige of His worship. They have been doing it now for well over fifty years. But in spite of the fact that two new generations have arisen in the meantime, all bombarded with anti-religious propaganda supported by the whole apparatus of government, education, scientific community, and cultural influence, there are still true believers to be found throughout the Communist world. Under the circumstances in which these believers live, they don't play a very great role in the societies of their countries, but they believe in God. In whatever way they can, they worship God, sometimes at the risk of their lives.

It doesn't take very much sense to see that God exists. It doesn't have to be proven, for deep down inside of each of us, we know it. No matter how hard we may try to educate it out of our system, when we get all through, we still know it. There is a God. That is not superstition. Superstitions begin when people try to picture God and what He is like. Superstitions begin when people try to picture God and what He is like. Superstitious ideas about God produce superstitious worship, and this can be found not only in primitive societies but also in the most intellectually developed countries in the world.

The answer to superstition is not atheism. That's just substituting one superstition for another. The most superstitious people in the world are those atheistic materialists who have made a God of things. They sanctify politics, they deify power, and they piously give their blessing to every sign of material progress. People who put their hope in things have to be afraid of every shadow, including their own. They wind up having so many unknown gods they don't know where to turn. It isn't that the modern atheistic or agnostic world hasn't got any religion, it has too much religion. The most fanatical religionists of our time are to be found in some of the most highly industrialized, richest, and most intellectual cultures of the world.

Say the word "God" and some people freeze. After all "God" is in bad taste. Say "Jesus" and you're really looked down upon. That's a name you just don't mention in polite company, because it's likely to challenge the sensibilities of some who think of themselves as "enlightened" and who feel that that kind of talk shouldn't be allowed.

St. Paul ran into that kind of thinking in Athens which was the intellectual capital of the world at that time. He was waiting there for Silas and Timothy to join him, and had been invited to speak at their public meeting place.

'Paul stood up in front of the meeting of the Areopagus and said: "Men of Athens! I see that in every way you are very religious. For as I walked through your city and looked at the places where you worship, I found also an altar on which is written 'To an Unknown God.' That which you worship, then, even though you do not know it, is what I now proclaim to you. God, who made the world and everything in it, is Lord of heaven and earth, and does not live in temples made by men. Nor does he need anything that man can supply by working for him, since it is he himself who gives life and breath and everything else to all men. From the one man he created all races of men, and made them live over the whole earth. He himself fixed beforehand the exact times and the limits of the places where they would live. He did this so they would look for him, and perhaps find him as they felt around for him. Yet God is actually not far from any one of us; for

'In him we live and move and exist.'

It is as some of your poets have also said,

'We too are his children.'

"Since we are God's children, we should not suppose that his nature is anything like an image of gold or silver or stone, shaped by the art and skill of man. God has overlooked the times when men did not know, but now he commands all men everywhere to turn away from their evil ways. For he has fixed a day in which he will judge the whole world with justice, by means of a man he has chosen. He has given proof of this to everyone by raising that man from death!" (Acts 17:22-31 TEV)

Paul picked these people up where they were. "You are very religious," he said. Some of them must have nodded their heads in agreement, and others probably smiled because they didn't think of themselves as being very religious. Paul pointed to their places of worship, which today would include not only churches, but banks, universities, political platforms, sports arenas, golf clubs, and a good many homes. You can tell what people worship by their devotion. If a man is devoted to his bank account, to his hobby, or to football, then that is what he worships. That is his god. Get in the way of that superstition and you disturb his whole life. He'll get upset and you'll hear about it. There are many gods and lords in this world of ours.

Paul drove right into the heart of all that religion. ". . . As I walked through your city and looked at the places where you worship, I found also an altar on which is written, 'To an unknown God.' " The presence of such an altar in an intellectual community might seem strange, but it was natural and appropriate. The mark of an intellectual in our time has often come to be that studied skepticism, that urbane irreverence, that seculiar piety which offers smiling deference when you talk about faith, and that ceaseless quest for truth which steadfastly refuses to admit that any truth can ever be found and never permits a man to say yes or no to anything. Whether those educated Athenians erected their altar to "an unknown god" to appease one they might have forgotten otherwise or whether they were paying sardonic lip service to the whole religious idea makes little or no difference. There the altar stood, a monument preserved today in the words of St. Paul.

"That which you worship, then," he said, "even though you do not know what it is, is what I now proclaim to you." He had something for everybody to know. He had found it out for himself some years before, and the finding made him the man he was. It put him on the road to salvation instead of the road to nowhere. It gave him the reason to be. It was true, and he knew it firsthand. Paul had met Jesus Christ, and it had changed his whole life.

"Even though in the past I spoke evil of him, and persecuted and insulted him. But God was merciful to me, because I did not believe and so did not know what I was doing. And our Lord poured out his abundant grace on me and gave me the faith and love which are ours in union with Christ Jesus. This is a true saying to be completely accepted and believed: Christ Jesus came into the world to save sinners. I am the worst of them, but it was for this very reason that God was merciful to me, in order that Christ Jesus might show His full patience with me, the worst of sinners, as an example for all those who would later believe in him and receive eternal life. To the eternal King, immortal and invisible, the only God—to him be honor and glory forever and ever! Amen." (1 Tim. 1:13-17 TEV)

Now that's worship. Worship is not just words. Too many of us have been satisfied with the words of worship, and have hardly worshiped at all. Worship is action. It is an attitude of the heart taking in a man's intellect, his lips, hands, feet, everything. Worship is the expression of a man's life. More than anything else, it tells us what kind of men we are. Paul had received life from Jesus. What he had been before was more like death than life. But when he met Jesus, life flooded in upon him. He kept saying, "Jesus is alive!" It kind of surprised people to hear that. Jesus had died. Paul said He had died for the sins of the world and he found that out for himself when he met Jesus alive. Jesus was raised from the dead by the glory of His Father. This was great good news, and Paul had to tell it. Jesus was declared to be the Son of God with power. *He lives.* He really does.

That being true, God has something to say to our world. "God who made the world and everything in it, is Lord of heaven and earth, and does not live in temples made by men." Worship is not restricted to time or place. "Nor does he need anything that men can supply by working for him, since it is he himself who gives life and breath and everything else to men." He does not need our worship to survive. "From the one man he created all races of men, and made them live over the whole earth. He himself fixed beforehand the exact times and the limits of the places where they would live. He did this so they would look for him and perhaps find him as they felt around for him." Looking for God, men prove themselves to be far more intelligent and far more sensitive to their own position in the world than by acting as if He does not exist.

"Yet God is actually not far from anyone one of us; for 'in him we live, and move and exist.' It is as some of your poets have also said, 'We too are his children.' ' " Poets have been able to see things which have escaped others of short vision.

"Since we are God's children, we should not suppose that his nature is anything like an image of gold or silver or stone, shaped by the art and skill of men." That goes for all the modern idols as well. You can't make God out of youth and you can't find God in the worship of progress. "God has overlooked the time when men did not know, but now he commands all men everywhere to turn from their evil ways."

Why now? Because Jesus Christ has come. His story is part of our history. The man Jesus lived and died; He gave His life for all of us. There is forgiveness and life through faith in Him, because He is the Son of God and the Savior of the world. That happened, and now everything is changed.

Jesus rose from the dead, and He is alive. Everyone and everything in this world of ours is headed toward a rendezvous with Him. "God has fixed a day, in which He will judge the whole world with justice, by means of a man He has chosen. He has given proof of this to everyone by raising that man from death!"

You can feel the worship of it. Its a fact of history, and what a fact it is! That day is fixed when God is going to judge the whole world with justice, and that is when the risen Christ returns. Proof? Everyone has it. God raised Him from the dead.

The church worships Him. It does not worship its own humanity, or its own ritual, or its own buildings, or the silver, the gold, the stone, the arts, the ingenuity of man. It worships Jesus Christ. Worshiping Him, it worships God. The church celebrates. It celebrates life, not its own life, but the life of Jesus Christ. Whatever there is of life in the church today comes from Him. Too much of what is called life in the church today comes from Him. Too much of what is called life in the church resembles death. Some of it is outmoded and some of it is just emptiness. I am afraid that many people simply go through the motions without any idea of what real life is all about. It is always life in Christ wherever the church has real life.

The worshiping church has forgiveness, like His forgiveness. It has love, like His love. It has a healing hand, like His hand. It has a warm encouragement, like His voice. The worshiping church disdains the politics of power, like the disdain of Jesus for the keepers of mere human traditions. The church has faith, like His confidence in His Father. It has joy, like the joy of Him who endured the cross, forgetting about the shame, and now sits at the right hand of His Father. In the worshiping church there is celebration, with tongues of fire marking the coming of the Spirit of God. The church celebrates life, His life.

Jesus is the revelation of God. Revelation is the means by which God reaches out to us; worship is our response to His reach. Because of Jesus, the church worships God.

T.S. Eliot said it this way: "Those who would deny thee could not deny, if thou didst not exist." The first move is God's, He made it. The second move is ours and we make that when we worship Him in spirit and in truth, Him in whom we live, move and have our being.

We are never more human than when we worship Him. We are men, He is God. He sent His Son to die for our sins, and He raised that Son from death. We need that Savior, and we need His forgiveness. We need His life. We are men, and that's why we worship Him. We worship Him in joy. "Make a joyful noise to God . . . sing the glory of his name (Ps. 66:1,2 RSV). Sing to the Lord a new song, sing to the Lord all the earth! (Ps. 96:1 RSV) Is any cheerful? Let him sing praise" (James 5:13 RSV). That's the worshiping church.

19

The Fellowship of Joy

And not only so, but we also joy in God through our Lord Jesus Christ, by whom we have now received the atonement. (Rom. 5:11 KJV)

These words originally came from St. Paul but it is a note most people don't expect to find in the church. To a lot of people, the church is supposed to be a rather somber or at least solemn place. Religious people are supposed to be known more for their seriousness than for the brightness of their smiles. After all, who can be profound and jump for joy at the same time?

"I can," says St. Paul. "For when we were still helpless, Christ died for the wicked, at the time that God chose. It is a difficult thing for someone to die for a righteous person. It may be that someone might dare to die for a good person. But God has shown us how much he loves us; it was while we were still sinners that Christ died for us! By his death we are now put right with God; how much more, then, will we be saved by him from God's wrath. We were God's enemies, but made us his friends through the death of his Son. Now that we are God's friends, how much more will we be saved by Christ's life!" These are very profound thoughts that led St.

Paul to a tremendous conclusion: "But that is not all; we rejoice in God, [we exult in God, we glory in God,] through our Lord Jesus Christ, [by whom we have this atonement, from whom we have received reconciliation,] who has now made us God's friends" (Rom. 5:6-11 TEV).

We can almost visualize St. Paul telling his listeners about Jesus. He is not the little, dark, scowling and bitter religionist some have made him out to be. At one time, he might have been that, but not now! He might still be little and dark, but not scowling and bitter. There is a friendliness in his approach; there is an attractiveness about him, a politeness in his eyes, a sunny expression on his face, and a warmth in his voice.

Something had happened to him, he had found Jesus, and that changed everything! "We jump for joy in God through our Lord Jesus Christ," he kept saying, "by whom we have now received the great thing, the atonement for our sins, reconciliation with God, and friendship with our Father, once alienated by our sins and now reconciled to us by the death of His Son. We joy in God through our Lord Jesus Christ. In Him we have atonement."

When we look around us in a lot of churches these days, we have to say to ourselves that people certainly must have forgotten something. People gathered in the churches seem so often to be gloomy, hostile to one another, suspicious of most, eager to find fault rather than to forgive, so solemn, so whisperingly quiet, so afraid to let themselves go, so unhappy. Our churches seem to be such unhappy places. What has happened? It must be that church people have really forgotten something. Could it be that they really don't believe what they are supposed to be celebrating and are afraid others will find it out? They seem to hide behind walls in the fear that someone or something will get to them. They seem to be on the defensive and that's a sign of insecurity and fearing the worst.

St. Paul wasn't like that at all. He said the worst could come and I don't care. I've got someone who will carry me through thick and thin. What can bother me, if God is for me? If God is for us, who can be against us? The God who gave us His own Son surely is not going to withhold from us any good thing. In this world of ours, come life, come death, come anything, He is a steadfast friend. By His death, Jesus dealt with the great issues of life and of death. He overcame and now in Him there is only life. That being the case, we joy in God through Jesus by whom we have now received this magnificent atonement.

Recently, I heard a story about a couple of friends engaged in a conversation about the subject of joy. One man said, "You know, I think the pastor last Sunday was trying to tell us that we are not as happy as we should be. I have been thinking the same thing. I think he's right. If we really took seriously all of God's promises, we would be happy and we would show it more." The second man commented, "There are all these problems pressing in on people. It has colored our whole mood. There is danger in the Middle East situation; it looks like a depression is right around the corner, and the world seems to be ready to collapse. To be happy today you almost have to be ignorant or stupid."

If we ignore the evil in the world, the problems people have, the racial hatreds and the personal hostilities, the starvation and degradation of the world's poor, the bloody violence and the malice that jabs a knife in the back, the brainlessness and heartlessness of world power, I guess we could be happy after a fashion. That kind of happiness is very superficial and will receive a rude awakening.

I have seen parents crack up and go to pieces when a boy or girl of theirs went wrong, bringing embarrassment and disgrace upon the family. They adored and spoiled their children, putting all their eggs in that one basket. When that dream exploded, their whole world blew up with it. I have seen that same kind of thing happen to men who put all their eggs in the basket of business. Businesses can fail in spite of mighty efforts, and thoughts of suicide can prevail. Happiness can be a very fragile thing, here today and gone tomorrow.

Many of us confuse happiness with pleasure. Happiness might be a good steak dinner, two weeks in the Caribbean, having that cute blonde or handsome brute smile at us, winning a new car, being young and in shape, enjoying ecstatic pleasures. One day, all of a sudden, we begin to get pains across the chest, or a good friend lets us down, or we lose our job, and then the whole picture changes. Happiness goes right out the window.

St. Paul was not impressed with the situations most people call happiness. He was talking about joy, deep down inside, outlasting misfortune, and not afraid of anything. This kind of joy is as present at the beginning of a good dinner as at the end. It is present at the beginning of a great vacation and after it's all over. It is present when the new car is delivered and when the car breaks down.

The kind of joy that St. Paul was talking about was that exultant quality in the early Christians that so much impressed and puzzled their pagan neighbors. It was different from anything that marked ordinary human life. Pleasure is one thing, joy is another. Pleasure, when chosen wisely and used in moderation, may do much to mitigate the rigors of life, but it can never create the atmosphere with which joy surrounds the man who has found it. Pleasure is as surface and temporary as the cause which calls it forth. Joy has an enduring quality. It is a state sustained by abiding sources of spiritual renewal and can't be taken away. It is inseparable from an experience of a proper relationship to God. In dependence on God we discover the secret of creative power and we master the disciplines of humble and happy service. That is why we rejoice in God. The genuine Christian is persuaded that only in Him can we find the wellspring of joy. The Christian is convinced that he cannot attain the requisite fellowship with God except through Jesus. Apart from Jesus we lack the knowledge of God which enables us to exult. He has not only shown us the Father, but He has made possible that reconciliation without which there can be no joy.

Our modern world has unconsciously incorporated a fatal error in its thinking, namely that modern life has outgrown its need for God and the Christian interpretation of life. Taking science as the key model, modern man claims that slowly he is gaining mastery over life. He is being freed from former bondages, and ultimately he will know a human quality of life that has never been achieved in the past.

That kind of thinking has also infected some assemblies of Christians. Some theologians and influential leaders of churches, both clerical and lay, have adopted an entirely secular view of life in which the role of God has become almost nonexistent. They may go through some religious forms, but these forms are empty of meaning. It is not so much that God becomes unimportant, but that they lose their way. The young offspring of modern secular man turn frantically to occult mysticism, drugs, outlandish Eastern religions, communes, almost anything, in order to find meaning in life.

When it comes right down to it, this is the reason for the unhappiness of the modern world, where people were supposed to be happier than they had ever been before. Man has cut himself off from the source of joy. Joy is there, just as it always has been, but man can't seem to find it. It isn't so much that he can't, but that he won't. He doesn't want to find it. People fight God. Previous generations did it, and found only unhappiness. People do it today, people like us. We fight off God. We hold Him at arm's length, we try to get along without Him. We treat God as if He were an outmoded idea which we somehow have outgrown. The truth is, without God, and without hope in the modern world, we are losers.

A lot of us suddenly are beginning to wake up to our lostness, our lack of someone to believe in, our failure to find joy. Where are we going to find that real faith, real love, and real joy, if we don't find it in church? How are we going to find it in our church, if it's not there? How can it be there, if our individual church has no real grip on God, if it doesn't know and love Jesus, if it no longer proclaims forgiveness and life through Jesus, if joy in these realities has been given up for some other moral or ethical philosophy which produces tidy but only temporary results?

To know joy, we must know what life is all about. Then we can live while things go wrong on the surface. We can bear the load when things collapse. We can keep on going even when we feel overwhelmed. I know joy because I know Jesus. I have received and continue to receive forgiveness and life from Him. Forgiveness always involves sacrifice, and Jesus sacrificed His life for mine. We ordinary men inflict suffering, often on the innocent, and only one who was innocent of all sin could take that ultimate suffering for sin, pay the price of its guilt, the terrible effect of sin on all of us. Only one could do that and He did.

A moping, sad and frustrated church body is one that doesn't know the meaning of atonement, doesn't know how to proclaim forgiveness. If it doesn't know how to do that, how can it bring joy to the world? There isn't anything our world needs more today than churches that are happy in their faith, happy in their love, happy in their joy of knowing and proclaiming Jesus. We can't have happy churches unless they are peopled by those who know Jesus as Lord and Savior.

The fellowship of joy will be ever present whenever the Good News of Jesus is proclaimed and lived. We can't blame our churches for the lack of joy, for after all *we* make up our churches. Our churches will become outstanding fellowships of joy when more and more of us come to consciously receive and accept Jesus as Savior and Lord.

20

The Fellowship of Prayer

Verily, verily, I say unto you, Whatsoever ye shall ask the Father in my name, he will give it to you. Hitherto have ye asked nothing in my name: ask, and ye shall receive, that your joy may be full. (John 16:23-24 KJV)

Ever since these words were spoken, wherever there have been gatherings of Jesus' disciples, wherever the church has really been the church of Jesus, the church has been a church of confident and expectant prayer. Wherever the gospel has been preached and lived, the church has believed and seen the fulfillment of Jesus' words: "Whatsoever ye shall ask the Father in my name, he will give it to you . . . that your joy may be full."

Prayer is not the dreary exercise some have made it out to be, nor is it the thing one does when nothing else works. There are some of us who turn to prayer only when we are down and out, or feeling sorry for ourselves, or when our hopes for glory, advancement or happiness don't turn out.

Jesus understands people in trouble, because He knew all about trouble himself. He knew His Father and turned to Him in times of trouble and times of tranquility. Knowing God is a fantastic experience. Jesus kept telling his listeners, "My Father knows me, and I know Him.'' This is not merely something for theologians to argue about, it is a practical fact of great importance to us ordinary people. Jesus knew God as His Father. Jesus came not only to show us the Father, but to hook everyone of us up to God. He suffered to bring us to God. He conquered for us the hostility, the stubbornness, and the fear that would drive us away from God. While we were yet enemies, He died for us; now by His life we are saved. His first followers kept saying to people ''Believe it, and be saved, everyone of you!'' And the same message still holds true for us today.

God speaks, and a lot of us don't listen. Then we wonder why He doesn't listen when all of a sudden we get the urge to pray. There are others of us who seem to think we're doing God a favor by praying to Him. A lot of people say to me, ''I prayed, but God wasn't listening.'' I believe it.

Anybody would agree that in business, school, or marriage, communication is a two-way street. If we want someone to listen to us, we have to be ready to listen to him. If whenever someone speaks to us our response is a vacant stare, then it is almost an insult to expect him to listen whenever we open our mouths. We talk to others only when we want to take them over for all they're worth. God is not stupid; He knows the score and we can't take Him over with that con job of pretending to do Him a favor by throwing Him a prayer now and then.

What good is a telephone in our home if it isn't hooked up to the lines? We could try to make a call until we're blue in the face and we wouldn't even get a dial tone. That is what a lot of us are complaining about when we say ''I prayed, but God didn't listen.''

Jesus is the one who hooks the line up between heaven and earth. He died to bring forgiveness and He lives to heal all the hurt. When we begin to listen to Jesus, to trust Him, the lines get connected and friendly communication with the Father is ours to have and enjoy. This is what Jesus was telling us when He told us, ''Whatsoever you ask the Father in my name, He will give to you. Ask in My name, and you will receive and you'll find out what joy is all about.''

There is a story about a young father who sat grimly through the funeral service of his four-year-old son. As he heard the opening words of the service, "I know that my Redeemer lives," he muttered under his breath, "God, I'll get back at you for this." It was an authentic human reaction. I've seen people react that way when they are overcome by terrible tragedy and suddenly come face to face with a fact of life they previously ignored. Like it or not, we have to deal with God. We can try to avoid Him but sooner or later we come to know that He is. We may not know Him, but we know that He is. That young father didn't realize it at the time, but he was closer to God right then than he had been for a long time. Later on that father said, "It was a foolish thing to say, I suppose. How could I ever get even with God? But it was honest. It was the way I felt, and it cleared the atmosphere to get it all off my chest. When I came to myself, I saw that death does have to fit into some kind of framework and only God can absorb that. In time I came to know His mind. I know now that my Redeemer does live.''

A lot of people aren't angry at God at all. They couldn't care less. The whole style and pace of modern life keeps them so occupied they don't have time to think about God. Actually most of these people, and we may be one of them, are caught in a crisis of faith. We would like to really believe in God, but don't think we can. We convince ourselves that to believe in God, and let that belief influence our lives, isn't quite the thing to do and remain modern. If we concede that God cares about us, we have to then care about Him and that goes against the grain of modern thought that teaches we should believe only in ourselves.

It is popular today to call upon science in support of this kind of independence, as if science has somehow destroyed God or rendered Him useless. Science hasn't done any such thing. People who won't pray because they think it's unscientific really don't understand science at all. Science doesn't claim that the investigation of God is its job at all; science tries only to understand the physical universe. When scientists try to use the tools of their trade to talk about God, they are like orthodontists trying to build a bridge across a great river. But that's impossible. God is not just a force, He is a person. That is what Jesus came to show us. God is a Father whose children are lost. He does everything to get them back again, even if it means giving His own life to do it. That is exactly what Jesus did. He shows the way back to be one again with the Father.

In Jesus, God invites us to communicate with Him. Come on, He says, talk to me through my Son. Jesus is our connection, come to me through Him. Don't worry about your problems, talk to me about them. I'll help you to their solution. This is really the reverse of the question a lot of us ask: What's the good of praying? And then we proceed to worry ourselves to death, as if worrying will solve our problems. The disciples of Jesus learned the joy of prayer. One of them said: "Cast all your care upon Him; for He will take care of you." That is exactly how it works. If we trust God we knock the stuffing out of our worries. Jesus says, "Ask in My name and you will receive and you will be full of joy." What Jesus says is this: "I know My Father and He knows me. Come to the Father in my name and you will find Him to be your Father too. He really loves you. You'll find that out for yourself when He answers your prayer through Me for your joy will be full."

Prayer is the exercise of our spiritual muscles. If we haven't been exercising them lately, we may find it a little painful at first. We begin by being honest with ourselves, not pretending but being natural with God. He isn't impressed with our pious powers of expression. He wants us to be ourselves. If we ask in Jesus' name, then we will receive.

All we have to do is to be natural, be ourselves. There is no special religious language that has to be used. If we were on the telephone with God, what would we say? We would probably feel a little flustered at first, with Him on the other end of the line. But all we would have to do is talk to Him about the things that have been worrying us, the things that have been eating at us, the things we would like to get off our chests. We can talk to Him about ourselves, we can talk to Him about others, mentioning them by name. We should let Him know that we have the courage to talk to Him because we have confidence in His Son, Jesus. That's good for us to remember, and it pleases Him to hear us say it. Jesus tells us that whatever we ask the Father in His name, the Father will give us.

We should have freedom in prayer, to feel free to say what we think. We should also feel free to use the words of someone else's prayer if they say what we want to say. A lot of us find the Psalms helpful in this regard. If we enjoy the gift of praying in other tongues, then the exercise of that gift should also be brought into use.

There are thousands of prayer meetings around that we can participate in to help us in our prayer. Wherever people pray with one another in the name of Jesus, the Holy Spirit is powerfully present and things begin to happen. If we want to experience joy instead of the gloom, dreariness, and barrenness of life without God, then we shouldn't be afraid, we should go and find out for ourselves. It could be the beginning of a renewed and exciting relationship with the Father.

I have come across some people who claim to know God but seldom if ever do they pray to Him. Sorry, folks, but that's not knowing God, that's only knowing about Him. There is no substitute for knowing God. That's where the joy comes in, knowing Him, having Him as an intimate friend, being sure of His forgiveness, looking to Him for what is really good in life, trusting Him to see things through, enjoying His presence, His nearness, His help. If any man is in Christ, that is what he is. He is a new man, with new life, new hopes, new dreams. He is a man with new desires and a new power for victorious living.

If anyone tries to tell me that it can't happen to them, I don't want to hear it. It can happen to anyone who is willing. If I can have it, anyone can. He talks to all of us when He says: "Whatever you ask the Father in my name . . . you will receive, that your joy may be full."

There is no better time than the present to take Jesus, to take Him at His word. Ask in His name and you will receive, and in the asking and in the receiving, you will find joy. Let us pray for ourselves, for others, in the name of Jesus. If we pray in the atoning name of Jesus, accepting Him as our Savior and receiving His forgiveness, at that moment we become full and alive members of His fellowship, for the church is the assembly of those throughout the world who trust Him and call upon His name. "Ask in my name," Jesus says, "and you will receive . . . that your joy may be full."

21

The Spirit and This Age

These things I have spoken to you, while I am still with you. But the Counselor, the Holy Spirit, whom the Father will send in my name, he will teach you all things, and bring to your remembrance all that I have said to you. (John 14:25,26 RSV)

"That's the way the cookie crumbles" is the typical manner our world speaks about the frustrations of human life. It is a rather pessimistic way of regarding things. There is absolutely nothing you can do to change things as they are. If our world is going to fall apart, there is nothing any of us can do about it. So why even try?

There are others who map out big plans and develop great patterns for a brave new world or a great society. But these utopias people plan never seem to come about. Sooner or later we find out that thinking does not bring about reality simply as a result of thinking. Are the pessimists right? Is there no possibility of change? The question is being asked today by many sensitive people. For many of them this block of time is empty and void of anything meaningful, of all joy and life. Something important is missing.

All over this world in crisis, many are agreeing with those who say that something is missing. It is missing in the political world, the schools, business, and even many of the churches. The Spirit is missing, that's what. Everything else is there, except the Spirit to make it alive and dynamic.

Jesus understands the emptiness of life and the desperation of mankind. He knows how it is, because He experienced it himself. He knew how lonely and helpless people can be. For people like that He gave His life, and for people like that *He lives today*. People like that He is ready to help. Our world, such as it is, needs to listen, really listen to Jesus.

Jesus said. "These things I have spoken to you while I am still with you. But the Counselor, the Holy Spirit, whom the Father will send in my name, he will teach you all things, and bring to your remembrance all that I have said to you."

No doubt many secularists and liberal Christians would be turned off by a message like this. All this talk about the Spirit of God sounds terribly impractical in a world where money is everything, progress is everything, power is everything, and status is everything. The Spirit of the living God that charismatic Christians are all excited about sounds like a child's dream in a "real" world. But to a world which has lost its way, God sends His Son to be its Savior. As God's chosen Man for *all* men everywhere, the Son of God forgives and gives life to all who have faith in Him. He sends His Spirit, and His Spirit is life. More than anything else our world needs His Spirit.

The Spirit of God, the Spirit Jesus promised, came to the world at Pentecost and continues to come all the time as evidenced by revival movements throughout the ages and the present restoration of New Testament Christanity in the charismatic renewal. Christ is present all over the world in His Spirit, His living and breathing Spirit. His Spirit that gives life and faith is present to and in the world. The world may pay Him little attention and even some of the churches may ignore Him, but the Spirit is doing a powerful work.

Where do we think the signs of new life are coming from all over the once-dying Christian world? There is a renewal of interest in the Scriptures, a renewal of genuine worship, a renewal of faith, a renewal of fellowship and New Testament forms. How is it that miracles are abounding again? The Holy Spirit is being poured out upon a needy world. The Pentecostal movement, or charismatic renewal, is one of the means by which God is building His temple and renewing the face of the earth.

As Jesus said, His Spirit is the Spirit of truth. Truth is unvarnished, objective reality. It is things as they actually are, undistorted and completely understood. Truth as a quality of mind is sincerity, which means positively the desire to take things as they are, and negatively the absence of all conflicting interest which might blur one's judgment. The Spirit brings both kinds of truth. He is the truth in the name of Jesus Christ. That truth becomes clear to everyone who has accepted the full gospel. That kind of truth takes some powerful doing, and the Spirit of God is doing it.

The Holy Spirit summons us to reverence, not for himself so much, but for Jesus. Jesus is the touchstone of truth. The Holy Spirit does not proclaim himself, He proclaims Jesus. Any so-called manifestation of the Spirit or ministry in the power of the Spirit that has not Jesus at the heart of it is no manifestation at all. The churches above all need to remind themselves of this fact and discern whom they allow to minister in their midst.

A good deal has been made of truth in our world. People quote that part of the statement of our Lord," the truth shall make you free." We see these words on the facades of public buildings. There is no ultimate truth when Jesus Christ is omitted. He said, "if you continue in my word, you will know the truth and the truth will make you free." The Holy Spirit is not just the Spirit of the world's creator, He is the Spirit of the world's Redeemer. That Redeemer is Jesus Christ. The Father sends His Spirit in the name of His Son. He teaches what the Son taught. No new prophecies, no new revelations are possible.

The Son was crucified and died. When He rose from the dead and was glorified, a new age began. It is the Age of the Spirit. That age will continue until everyone in the world has had a chance to see the things of God. "He will teach you all the things of God. He will teach you all the things and bring to your remembrance all that Christ had said and done." As a witness to Jesus, He tells the truth and nothing else really matters. That is why I convey this message. Like St. Paul, I don't preach about myself, but about the Lord Jesus. It is not my truth, and I have no particular power to convince you of its truth. The Spirit of God has that power. He is present and He speaks to hearts. This is His age, the age of the Spirit.

Jesus did not argue about God. He wasted no time in trying to prove the existence of God. No one needs to prove that. Everyone except a stubborn fool knows it is true. The only questions are who is He and what is He like? How does He feel towards us? Does He care? Yes, He does, says the Spirit. God is love and His love is made manifest in Jesus. Believe in Jesus and be saved from the spiritless emptiness of this age, be filled with His Holy Spirit and live! This is the main message and ministry of the Pentecostal movement, the charismatic renewal: receive the baptism with the Holy Spirit, be filled with the Spirit and you will have abundant life.

The love of God is active in the world. In spite of everything, God is love and His love is active. He wants to save people from themselves. He is working at it. His Spirit is alive, present, and active. He is at work in consciences, showing us who we are and where we stand. He is healing the divisions among all who call upon the name of Jesus. He is demonstrating the glory of God and the Word of God, Jesus who was raised from the dead by the glory of His Father. In Jesus there is forgiveness, healing, and wholeness.

The Spirit is calling all of us to a basic mission and ministry. That is the way the Spirit works. *He* declares Jesus Christ, everything in Jesus. "When the Spirit of Truth comes, he will guide you into all truth; for will not speak on his own authority, but whatever he hears he will speak, and he will declare to you the things that are to come" (John 16:13 RSV). The things to come when these words are spoken were the Crucifixion, the Resurrection, and the Ascension of Jesus. Jesus is the brightness of God's glory, and Pentecost is the breaking out of that glory upon the lives of little men and women like ourselves.

By the Spirit of God we hear and learn of Jesus. For our sake he made him to be sin who knew no sin, so that in him we might become the righteousness of God (2 Cor. 5:21 RSV). "Being justified freely by his grace through the redemption that is in Christ Jesus, whom God hath set forth to be a propitiation through faith in his blood, to declare his righteousness for the remission of sins that are past, through the forbearance of God" (Rom. 3:24,25).

The whole word of God is a declaration of the Spirit about things that are and things that are to come. They all come true in Jesus. The message of all truth in Jesus, after everything is said and done, is that forgiveness is for everybody, conservative and liberal, charismatic and non-charismatic, Catholic and Protestant. This is what the Spirit is saying and this is His age.

The greatest happening in life is not the appearance of some new great prophet on the scene but the transformation of ordinary people like ourselves by the power of the Spirit of Christ. That is what is happening and that is why the charismatic renewal is so remarkable. The main event is not some particular person or persons with soul-stopping ministries, but that Spirit-filled and Spirit-directed ministry is being returned to all the members of the Body.

This is His age. The power of God is demonstrably present, His Spirit is alive and acting. We must have faith in Jesus and live. We must become a part of this age of truth and not stand apart from it as many are doing because of theological prejudices and stances. The Spirit of God shares Jesus Christ, not theology, with ordinary people like ourselves and life becomes new again, with a new outlook, a new disposition, and new power. We in turn must share Jesus, only Jesus and His Holy Spirit so that His life and His power will really renew the face of the earth.

As a Roman Catholic and a charismatic I have prayed and hoped that the pope would someday recognize and officially declare the charismatic renewal in the Catholic Church to be an authentic work of the Holy Spirit in the present age. On October 16th, 1974, my prayer was answered as evidenced by the following news release by Kevin Ranaghan through the Charismatic Renewal Services:

Pope Paul VI said today that the Church can have a new abundance of charismatic gifts and that the prodigy of Pentecost has to continue in the Church and in the world. Speaking to thousands at his weekly general audience, the Holy Father specifically recommended the work of Cardinal Leon Josef Suenens in his new book "A New Pentecost?" In this book, which will appear in English in March, Cardinal Suenens examines the outpouring of the Holy Spirit in the Church with special reference to the contemporary Charismatic Renewal.

The Pope, teaching on the necessity of grace, spoke of the illusion of those who say they have no need of God and who declare their self sufficiency. He stressed man's fundamental need for God and for the infusion of grace, the gifts of God and the power of the Holy Spirit. After describing the work of The Spirit in saving, sanctifying grace, the Pope went on to speak of charisms such as miracles which flow from the superabundance of the Lord and which enrich, enliven, and strengthen the Church and enable it to be more clearly visible in the world. The Pope said that the charismatic gifts attract the attention of the world to the power of the Gospel.

I see it happening. We live in the Age of the Spirit. Praise God!

22

The Renewed Church

For through the living and eternal word of God, you have
been born again as the children of a parent who is immortal,
not mortal. (1 Pet. 1:23 TEV)

St. Peter addressed these words originally to the people of his
day who had become Jesus people and they come to us ordinary
people of today who have found Jesus. These Jesus people are
found all over the world today withstanding the pressures of
modern life. If the Jesus people of the apostolic age needed this
reminder, then the Jesus people of today need it too. "Through the
living and eternal word of God you have been born again as the
children of a parent who is more than mortal. God the Father
himself."

A lot of people who are seeking reality neither in Jesus nor His
church wonder what it is like to find it in Jesus and His church. If
they were to ask the question, "What is it like?" of someone who
has had the experience of Jesus' living reality and who is joined to a
fellowship sharing that reality, the answer would probably be, "It
is like being born again, getting a new lease on life, acquiring a
whole new attitude, becoming a new creation, and the whole thing
comes from God the Father himself." That is not only what it is

like, that is what it is.

All of it began with God. St. Peter tells us that what it cost to set us free from the worthless manner of life we received from our ancestors, was not something that loses its value like silver and gold. We were set free by the costly sacrifice of Jesus, who was the lamb without a defect or spot. Through Him we believe in God, who raised Him from death and gave Him glory; so our faith and hope are fixed on God.

Something happens when people get to know Jesus, really to know Him. It is not the mere repetition of some half-understood slogans, the kind of thing with which too many people call themselves Christians seem to be very well satisfied. It has to be said that half-hearted Christianity never encouraged anyone to learn to know Jesus and to follow Him.

There isn't any force in that kind of Christianity and those outside the church see it right away; often they see it better than people inside the church. So many in the church are satisfied with the mere profession of Christianity that doesn't have any practical results in their personal lives. That is not the kind of knowing Jesus that Peter talks about. "Now that by your obedience to the truth you have purified yourselves and have come to have a sincere love for your fellow believers, love one another earnestly with all your hearts. For through the living and eternal word of God you have been born again as the children of a parent who is immortal, not mortal" (1 Pet. 1:22,23 TEV).

What the world needs today is a church that is newborn, that is renewed. The world has had its fill of churches that try to satisfy the hunger of people with theological piffle and sociological jargon. The world is completely turned off by churches that argue among themselves as to who is first in the kingdom while it hungers for the life-giving message of Jesus. Building programs, bigger budgets, liturgical innovation, and theories of social action, useful as they may be, do not hold within themselves the answer to the world's problems. The inner workings and apparatus of the church is just a means to an end. Of what value is it if the church has no end, no aim, no goal, no purpose that consumes its energies with passion for genuine accomplishment? What good is the church if it just idles along, as the world idles along, with little to go on and nowhere to go? Wherever the church consciously and experimentally realizes it is the Body of Jesus, it is alive, reborn, and renewed and people are drawn to it. This is the kind of church we read about in the Acts of the Apostles. The New Testament apostolic church was peopled by those who had experienced Jesus and were alive with the power of the Holy Spirit. Before these people came to know Jesus, they were pawns, victims, playthings of the disintegrating forces of the world, its fragmented purpose and cruelty. After they came to know Jesus, they had solid purpose and clear vision, and the power of the Spirit with which to tackle the difficult, the intricate, and the impossible trials of life. Their lives, before experiencing Jesus, had been a cycle of blasted hopes and disillusionments, of error and random commitments; now they were part of something, indeed, part of someone. They were born again by the eternal word of God and they really knew themselves to be the children of the immortal God.

Life in Jesus is exciting and joyous. He gives those who receive Him a new way of looking at things, a new way of thinking and acting. Life in Jesus is a constant and open challenge, bright and rich with possibilities, and at the same time, it is secure, rooted in a victorious, reigning and everlasting Lord. His life becomes the life of all those who follow Him. This is the Father's plan for us. The church is not just another social institution that appears on the scene for a short time and then dies. The church lives on, in spite of some of the people who belong to it. It lives on because it is the Body of Jesus, the suffering Son of God, now raised to power and glory.

The church lives by the word of God and the word of the Lord remains forever. The word of God lasts, it doesn't die. It is an abiding, living word. It is a remarkable word, come alive in a living person, Jesus Christ.

In times past, God talked to men at different times and in various ways through His prophets. Some were historians, others were poets; some were statesmen, others were farmers. God spoke through them to His people, stirring up new life to replace the old worn-out ways characteristic of our world. But now, He has spoken to the world in his Son Jesus. That is where the life is, in Jesus. In Him is life, and His life is the light of men. He died for sins, and sin is forgiven. He laid His life on the line, and in Him there is life for all. He cuts through all the moral chaos and mess of the world. The obedience of faith in Him brings life and the freedom to be His people. It is like being born again; it *is* being born again.

The purpose of the church of Jesus, the goal toward which it strives, is resurrection, like that of Jesus himself. Resurrection is coming alive after being dead. It is a renewal, and it happens through the word of God, the Good News of Jesus, offering forgiveness to a world that doesn't like to talk about its rebellion against Him and doesn't particularly want to be forgiven. Yes, He does forgive and continues to give life. That is the Good News and the mission of the church is first to live it and then preach it to the world.

People today crave something that will free them from their confusion. The contemporary scene shows they will try almost anything, from desperate schemes to self-help to the weirdest kinds of occult supernaturalism. Thank the Lord a growing number of people are discovering that only the word of God, the lively and life-giving Good News of Jesus, produces real change, real life, real hope, real joy and real courage.

Where do we find the word of God acting that way? We find it among people who are doers of the word, and not hearers only. They learn the lesson in what Jesus said: "My business is to do the will of Him who sent me." In doing the will of His Father, Jesus found strength and renewed resource for living and dying with confidence in His Father. The unadulterated word of God produces faith, faith produces love, and love can change the world. This kind of stuff belongs to people who use their spiritual muscles and don't allow them to grow slack from inactivity. They believe in, and live in, God's power.

There is nothing inactive or self-centered about those who are born again by the word of God; they have tuned in on Him and the sound can be heard whenever they open their mouths. They have seen God, and the light of that vision can be seen in their eyes. They crave the word of God as infants crave milk to stay alive.

The word of God, the Good News of Jesus, is the nutrient of the church. It always has been and always will be; that is why the Scriptures are so important to the church. They are not a club with which to beat the sheep over the head, they are the life-giving power of God, bringing Good News to a world needing salvation. The hearing and living of the word is the way to salvation and to life in all its abundance.

If we wonder what is wrong with the church today, this is it. Too many within the church are apathetic to the word of God. They are neutral, half-believing, half-faithful, half-loving, half-ready to hear the Good News, and half-interested in putting it into practice. That's why the church is half dead and half alive.

When the early Christians were baptized, they testified that they experienced new life and entered a new world. Jesus was born in them and the whole church was reborn. It was like Easter morning, when a man rose from the dead. Jesus was raised from the dead by the glory of His Father, and that is the way we walk in newness of life.

The word of God has the power to take hold of the world's ills and cure them. The word of God has the power to take hold of our personal ills and cure them. That is what the death of Jesus means for us. Jesus is the death of sin and guilt. His Resurrection and sending of the Holy Spirit opens a new door leading to a new life. Faith in Jesus works. It works new life and produces new attitudes.

It makes for new action in genuine love.

Where do we find that today? We find it in the church new-born, the church renewed. We must admit that not every member of the church is the best example of the new life in Jesus. Some don't have that new life operating at all, and some are just learning it. Some haven't grown up very much, and some have had their growth stunted. But there are others who are bursting with that new life. They don't care about power or prestige, they don't worry about popularity or unpopularity. They just love the Lord Jesus and are full of His life. They shine like lights in the darkness. They are good parents respected by their children; good neighbors always depended upon to do what is right in their communities. They are courageous and involved participants in their churches. They are the church reborn and renewed through the living and eternal word of God. They are children of a heavenly Father, and they don't feel like they have to parade the fact.

Our world needs Christians like that. They aren't just pious, they believe. They don't just say nice things, but they act to help others. The word of God is the key. If we crave salvation and rescue from the sordidness of life, we have to use that key. We can take it and open the door to life for ourselves. We can take it and open the door to a new beginning, a new life, new hope, new joy, and new power. They're ours for the asking.

We are asked to join ourselves to Jesus, for when we do that, no matter what tradition we come from, we receive new life and we are part of the renewed church.

When we take Jesus, we are part of a fellowship that cuts across lines of traditional demarcation. We become aglow with the Spirit, lovers of Jesus and of His church.

PART IV

JESUS AND THE FAMILY

23

What about Marriage?

Then the Lord God said, "It is not good that the man should be alone; I will make him a helper fit for him." (Gen. 2:18 RSV)

Is marriage as we know it on the way out? That question is being asked in utter seriousness, not only by crackpots who don't know what is going on, but also by thoughtful people who do know what's going on.

Marriage itself is being so weakened these days that the conclusion has been made that marriages are breaking up at about the same rate as they come into being. Statistics indicate that the divorce rate is about twenty-five per cent of the marriage rate. That means that one out of four marriages is breaking up in the world right now.

We can look at this situation in another way. There are about fifty million families in the United States. About five-hundred thousand of these marriages are in the process of breaking up at the present time. If we consider that the breakup of a family takes a couple of years, at most about one million of these fifty million families are proving to themselves and others that marriage can go on the rocks. One out of fifty is not quite as alarming as one out of four. It's still a bad situation.

There are other marriages which are in various stages of decay. There has been no legal divorce, but in effect, divorce has occurred even though everyone is still living in the same house. Such a situation encourages infidelity and other evils, often building a spirit of bitterness that poisons all of life.

Certain developments have affected family life. Families move around a good deal more today than they used to and they don't sink their roots nearly as deeply into the community as they once did. They don't know their neighbors and their neighbors don't know them. People live longer today than they used to. In the days of our grandparents it was not common for a marriage to last thirty years before one or both of the partners died. Today very many marriages could conceivably last fifty years. That's twenty years more of learning how to live together in mutual companionship or mutual bitterness, as the case may be. A lot of other factors, including employment of husband and wife in differing careers with different fields of interest, put increasingly greater pressures —for good or evil—on the marriage relationship.

It is not my purpose to attempt to cover every problem that may occur in a marriage. That would be material for a great many books. (*The Christian Family* by Larry Christenson is, I consider, the best in the field so far.) However, I make bold to write about marriage anyway, but only about those certain truths basic to every marriage. It is important for everyone to know and consider the foundation of marriage laid down in the second chapter of Genesis: "Then God said, 'it is not good that the man should be alone; I'll make him a helper fit for him.' "

When you think about it, it is quite a phenomenal idea. It influences human life more than any other single idea, any other human relationship. Man and woman, made for each other, that is God's idea. Whether you call it sex, love, or mutual attraction, it affects politics, business, education, recreation and just about anything else in human life that can be named.

It was God's idea that the relationship between two persons, man and woman, should be marriage. I know there are people with other ideas, but this is God's idea. People who have tried out the other ideas find they really don't work in the long run. Even in our modern world, there are examples of nations which tried out the idea of free love and the easy dissolution of marriage. It didn't, and doesn't, work. Most went back to the old idea, because it is the only one that works.

People can mess up almost any good idea. Leave it to them and they'll botch it all up. Marriage is too important an idea to be entered into thoughtlessly, as so many do, marrying in haste and repenting at leisure. It is too great an idea to expect it to work automatically without each of the partners working at it. When other people are included, nothing works automatically. People have to get together to make it work. That's the humanity of the whole business.

God has a pretty good idea of humanity. He understands man's need for companionship. Marriage is not the only way to meet that need, but it's a pretty good way. God made man and woman sexual beings, so that they could complement one another in their lives together. Probably no one appreciates that fact more than a wife or husband who have just lost their spouse in death. I've met a lot of people like that. Marriage made sense for them, and now a great deal of the sense has gone out of life for them. Bereaved women have frankly told me how much they miss their husbands, their companionship, their male sexuality, their good humor and good sense. Men have told me the same about their dead wives. Some of them admit they had wished they had recognized, appreciated and enjoyed the goodness of marriage more when their partners were alive.

There is no institution in all of society that has greater potential for satisfying the human need for companionship than the institution of marriage. Companionship in marriage is intimate, wherever there is real marriage; it is both physical and spiritual; it is God's great and good idea for the major part of humanity.

Human life is not a stagnant thing. It is always on the move. People change and they grow. It is God's idea that marriage should grow with them.

Marriage is necessary to human survival. Survival may not be the best reason for marriage, but marriage is survival together. Individual personal growth becomes a deeper enterprise when it is shared with the growth of another. Marriage is a team effort to help two individuals care for each other. All of human society depends on this intimate relationship. When it goes, society goes too. Is marriage on the way out? If it is, then society is on the way out too!

In a real marriage, husband and wife become more and more married as times goes on. A couple celebrating their twenty-fifth wedding anniversary can tell us all about it. They are more married now then they were on the day when they made their vows. Marriage is more than a legal contract. It is a sacred sign helping to cause what it symbolizes. It is a process of growing together in love, loyalty, and understanding. It's something to work at day by day, "until death do us part."

Marriage changes because people change. We are not the same today as we were on this same day last year. Two people make a marriage, and marriage changes with them. Some immature people never get used to this idea. They change, but they want their marriage to be what it was on their honeymoon. Some of them think they can recover that honeymoon feeling by changing partners. It never works. Most married couples will tell you that they are glad their marriage didn't stay where it was on their honeymoon. They know each other better now, understand each other better, have better sexual relationships, and love each other a great deal more. That's God's idea and that's how it works.

God is always available to help make it work. It's His idea and He wants it to work. Happy marriage is a gift from God, but it isn't handed to people on a silver platter. They have to work at it too. All too often marriages fail because people don't work at it. Marriage may be made in heaven, but it has to be worked out on earth.

People are not perfect. Those who think they are, are not good candidates for marriage. Perfect people had better go it alone without looking for help from anybody. When the time comes, of course, they will discover how imperfect they really are. In the meantime, they don't have to take it out on a partner in marriage, imposing their own perfections on somebody else.

A good marriage needs a lot of forgiveness. At times in every marriage, somebody has to say, "I'm sorry." Often it's the wife who says it first because that's the way wives are. Women generally understand human relationships better than men do. But men are foolish if they feel that they'll be less than masculine if they're the first ones to say, "I'm sorry." It takes a real man to do that. Happy marriages are two-way streets between real men and real women, conscious of their own imperfections and capable of forgiving one another.

That's God's idea. He knows how to forgive. It's the one reason Jesus came into the world. Jesus died for our imperfections, to make good for them. He died for all, that there might be forgiveness from God for all. Forgiveness is at the heart of the whole business. It is at the heart of family life. It's God's idea, and it works.

Marriage is a lifelong convenant of mutual love, faithfulness, and forgiveness. It is a picture, at it's best, of God's own family in the world. The Bible is always talking about God's faithfulness. He promises to love and He keeps that promise. We see it all in Jesus, God's Son. He is the living promise of God, His promise to the whole world, the promise of atonement, forgiveness and genuine life.

People who see that promise in Jesus, and accept it in faith, are received by God into His own family. They belong to Him. I guess that's why St. Paul compared God's family to a bride. Jesus is the groom. He loves that bride even though she may not always be attractive. He makes her lovely and beautiful, without a spot or wrinkle or any such thing. I've seen that same look on the face of a man contemplating this bride of fifty years on their golden wedding anniversary. To him she was as beautiful a bride now as she was the day they were married. Others may not think so, but he knows better. It wasn't glory for either one of them, but it was good. People being what they are, it's as good as anything in life can be. It's loyalty come to flower. It's God's idea, and it's beautiful.

A recent book on marriage says: "A happy family is not without problems; rather it's a family which has learned to handle it's problems." Accidents, illness, emotional upsets, and financial reverses do occur. They happen in the best families. The true test for a genuine marriage is how people take them, meet them, surmount them. That takes faith, faith in something more than yourself. It takes faith in God.

Happy families normally have some things in common: First, there's a feeling of love and affection between family members. Second, they hear each other out, are more ready to accept than to refute, supporting one another rather than undermining each other. Third, they have problems, but they continue to plan for the future. They combine practicality with idealism. Fourth, they engage in all kinds of activity and interests. They do not stifle one another in excesses of togetherness, but take pride and delight in individual accomplishments of parents and children inside and outside the home. Fifth, they have a capacity for humor, fun, and enjoyment. They reach out with exuberance and positive affirmation of the goodness of living.

There is another important feature of a happy family. Its members experience the presence of God in their homes with an unaffected and straightforward faith in Jesus. Faith has an incomparable transforming power to help family life attain its fulness. That's God's idea, too. It's His idea in Jesus. It's His idea, when people like us come to faith in Jesus, accept Him as Savior, and then follow His leading. It's His practical idea to bring about that total unity, which is according to His plan, for the experience of marriage.

24

What about Divorce?

Some Pharisees came to him and tried to trap him by asking, "Does our Law allow a man to divorce his wife for any reason he wishes?" Jesus answered, "Haven't you read this scripture? 'In the beginning the Creator made them male and female, and said, "For this reason a man will leave his father and mother and unite with his wife, and the two will become one." ' So they are no longer two, but one. Man must not separate, then, what God has joined together." The Pharisees asked him, "Why then, did Moses give the commandment for a man to give his wife a divorce notice and send her away?" Jesus answered "Moses gave you permission to divorce your wives because you are so hard to teach. But it was not this way at the time of creation. I tell you, then, that any man who divorces his wife, and she has not been unfaithful, commits adultery if he marries some other woman." (Matt. 19:3-9 TEV)

One of the signs of the breakdown of society today is the breakdown of the family. Another is the prevalence of divorce. The quotation above is very clear and shows us Jesus' mind about the question.

Actually, Jesus was talking more about marriage than about divorce. Be that as it may, it's a hard word for a loose age where people have been educated to think of life as purely the fulfillment of their own desires, even of the whims that come to them from moment to moment. There is little discipline in that kind of attitude, practically no respect for authority, including divine authority, and even less hope for stability, without which we cannot survive as human beings.

Just hearing what Jesus has to say about marriage and divorce will make some people laugh. They treat Him as a back number, out of touch with the world, having nothing to say to modern man who has gone far beyond that old, outdated, and outworn institution where one man takes one woman as his wife, and the two stay together, work together, and live together their whole lives. Jesus knows more about man than people know about themselves. He knows, as St. John says, what is in man. He knows what makes for human happiness, as far as happiness can be found by people living with human waywardness and human willfulness. He sees life whole, not in bits and pieces as we are often inclined to see it.

Only someone who views life as a collection of meaningless bits and pieces could ever look upon divorce as the way to happiness, as a satisfactory solution to human half-heartedness. When divorce takes place, something has gone wrong. It requires an unrealistic optimism to look upon something like that as a solution to a human problem. It is not the end of trouble. It's the beginning. Divorced people can tell us all about that. Divorce is not what it's cracked up to be. Marriage has a promise from God, divorce does not. Marriage brings a blessing, but who can say that about divorce?

There was a recent newspaper article entitled "Divorce is the tie that binds." The article was illustrated with a picture of a large cake decorated with the words "Happy Divorce," and it described a party held by a couple in honor of their recent divorce. The writer pointed out that marriages are like onions. They linger on. The article quoted a statement by Morton Hunt in his book *The World of the Formerly Married*; "Divorce is never really final. It is only nearly final." Over sixty per cent of divorcing people remain involved with each other for many years. People once married remain forever linked by experiences they have shared and by common memories that remain a permanent part of their personalities.

Why is there divorce? Jesus said divorce happens for the same reason that we have all the other problems in life. People are not what they ought to be. They mess things up, and they won't even admit that they have made a mistake. They try to justify themselves. We can abide people like that, when they live next door, but when they're in the same house they rub us raw. Let that situation go on, and it will grow worse. It becomes harder and harder to forgive. Self-justification on both sides becomes a way of life. The result is divorce, whether formalized by a court or not.

A review of a book directed to women who have been divorced recognized the fact that women in this situation are generally very depressed. They feel very sorry for themselves. The author tried to suggest some of the things they ought to be doing. He tells them how to manage their funds, how to engage in worthwhile activities, how to build a worthwhile basis for a new life. The reviewer of the book commented that it would have been a lot better if that advice had been given to the girl when she was eighteen and still unmarried rather than to a divorced woman at thirty-nine. Maybe, then, there would be fewer divorces.

Some marriage ceremonies call for a flower girl to walk down the aisle sprinkling rose petals, to symbolize the hope that the couple will enjoy a married life that is rosy and happy. Married life is not a bed of roses. Even roses have thorns and bugs. That's because two people are involved in a marriage, not two angels.

Some couples are on cloud nine when they first get married, and when they look at each other they see an angel. Pretty soon, though, the angel is transformed into a plain, ordinary, imperfect human being and joins the ranks of the large army of ex-angels.

167

There are some couples who couldn't live apart before they were married. Within six months they just can't live together.

That kind of situation is no joke. Anybody who has ever been divorced doesn't need a party or a cake to celebrate the event. Psychologists tell us that, next to death, divorce is the most traumatic event, the most emotionally injurious event, that can happen to any human being. It is like losing an arm, a leg, an eye, or a loved one. It is like standing at a grave. It is like burying your own life.

There are times when divorce seems to be the lesser of two evils. It is always an evil, however. It is not an easy solution, but develops rather into a difficult problem, especially when children are involved. You can divorce your spouse, but you can never divorce your children. The Roman Catholic church may allow separation of a married couple, but does not allow either of them to remarry because it believes that marriage cannot be dissolved; in these cases even legal civil divorce may be counseled, but always with the understanding that neither are free to remarry. The civil divorce is allowed only to avoid any legal complications.

When a couple cannot stand each other any longer, when their home life becomes a hell on earth, what are they to do? What did Jesus say? He is the Lord of heaven and earth and He ought to know. He came to reconcile people to God. That is about as difficult a reconciliation as can possibly be imagined. It may not look difficult to some people, but very often they are the ones who carry their hostility to God right into their graves. They never did manage it. They never knew what it meant to know God, to enjoy His grace, to have His forgiveness, to experience life as it was meant to be. They managed somehow, but they never found the deep satisfaction of living at peace with God and enjoying that peace with one another.

This does not mean that it is impossible to find God and to know His peace. He is close to us at this moment. Whenever we hear about Jesus, we are coming face to face with God. Jesus knows all about the human predicament. That is what took Him to His cross and to a borrowed grave. He knows all about that. He paid the price of human sin, human weakness, human degradation, and human dissatisfaction that rubs us raw. He paid the price, and now there is forgiveness for all that is human in every one of us.

Look at Jesus and we see the grace of God. The smiling face of God is in Jesus and that makes a difference in everything that is human. If we take the forgiveness of God in Jesus, if we accept it for ourselves by faith in Jesus, we would know all about that. We aren't perfect either. If we need forgiveness, then anyone who enters into relationship with us needs it too. People who really know the forgiveness of God are bound to show a forgiving spirit to one another. When that happens in a marriage, we have the beginning of something great. For most of us that's when marriage really begins.

It is not an easy way. It wasn't easy for Jesus, and it isn't easy for us either. Divorce may look like the easy way out, but actually it offers no chance at all to find a new beginning. Most of the time it just means more of the same.

Sure, He said men divorce their wives. Even Moses gave permission for that because people are so hard-hearted, so unready to listen to God, so hard to teach. But it was not this way at the time of creation. In the beginning the Creator made them male and female and said, ''For this reason a man will leave his father and mother and unite with his wife, and the two will become one.'' So they are no longer two, but one. Man must not separate them because God has joined them together.

When a marriage goes sour, reconciliation is by all means a better answer than divorce will ever be. The Bible says reconciliation comes from God. It is His hand reaching down to imperfect people, restoring, and producing new life.

At the heart of it all is His forgiveness. At the heart of that forgiveness is Jesus, suffering what we suffer, and not refusing to die for our sins. He gave himself as the Bible keeps saying, and the new life in Christ is to give yourself with the same unselfishness that characterizes Jesus.

At the heart of any marriage is giving. Men and women have to learn that. Most of us have to work at it because it doesn't come naturally. It is developed through exercise. The creative thing comes from God who made man and woman and said, "For this reason a man will leave his father and mother and unite with his wife, and the two will become one. So they are no longer two but one. What God has joined together, then let no man set apart."

The Pharisees, fine churchmen that they were, and practical men at that, were aware that some people just can't live with each other in marriage. Some of them ought not to have married in the first place. Some of them, for one reason or another, never will be able to make a go of marriage. There is such a thing as divorce in this world of ours, and even Moses allowed it.

Our Lord said, "Yes that's right, divorce is a fact of life. Any man, however, who divorces his wife, unless she has been unfaithful, and then marries some other woman, commits adultery." He did not mean that if a wife finds out her husband is going out with another woman or a husband learns that his wife is running around with another man, that divorce is the automatic solution to the problem. There is still forgiveness, even though it happens seventy times. That is the way God forgives, and that is the way we have to learn to forgive. The love of God should become a part of our bloodstream. I have seen Christian spouses forgive the worst sins and go on to make a marriage in spite of it all. It wasn't what it could have been, but it was a marriage. It takes work in faith and love.

Jesus had a heart for people even when they had been divorced. The burden of divorced people is heavy enough without having someone else rub salt into their wounds. Most of us don't know the whole story when a divorce takes place. It is not the time to be gossipy and suspicious; rather it is time to seek to understand, to offer help. When a marriage breaks up, people need help. When everything is falling apart, Christian people can help to pick up the pieces without being nosey. If people have been the victims of their own willfulness, there is still time to start a new way of life, the kind that Jesus alone can give.

Divorce is contrary to God's order. People who are divorced feel that too, deep down inside. The healing hand of God has something for them too and that is forgiveness and the promise of new life in Him. Here too people are not saved by rules, but by repentance and the open acceptance of God's goodness in Jesus.

Divorce is not the answer to a limping marriage. A clear head is a lot better. People say "love is blind." None of us can afford to be blind in that way. If our marriage is on the rocks, let's open our eyes and use the brain God gave us. Now is the time, not later when it's too late. Some say, "A fight a day keeps the doctor away." Now that's foolishness. A home is not meant to be a battleground. It is to be a refuge from the struggles of the day, a haven of peace, a bit of sunshine in the rain.

A good marriage requires plain honesty. Marriage is not just a legal contract for sexual activity. It is a covenant between two people who promise to stand by one another no matter what happens. Whenever I conduct the marriage ceremony, I hear the couple say to each other, "I promise to love you, to comfort you, to honor you and keep you in sickness and in health, and to forsake all others and to be faithful to you." These promises are important. There isn't anything more important than keeping faith. When faith goes, everything can go. As long as there is faith, everything can go, and still the bond will only grow stronger.

The answer to an unhappy marriage is not divorce. Divorce often leads to another unhappy marriage, leading to another divorce. That is not the answer. It is the end, rather than a new beginning. Marriage depends upon faith. It doesn't depend upon children either, although children bring a lot of joy to a marriage. In the final analysis, marriage depends upon faith; that's the secret.

Faith makes for a new beginning each day. Faith works by love, whenever Jesus is in that faith. Love may not be perfect, but it's still there. It's there wherever the love of God is there in Jesus.

This is not just religious faith. It is the kind of practical faith that makes a marriage. Faith in God, trust in Jesus, and faithfulness toward one another, all with love, make a man a husband and a woman a wife. That is more than mere religion, it is life.

25

What about Children?

As for you, my brothers, you were called to be free. But do not let this freedom become an excuse for letting your physical desires rule you. Instead, let love make you serve one another. For the whole Law is summed up in one commandment: "Love your fellowman as yourself. (Gal. 5:13,14 TEV)

As Christians, we must take the risk of raising children, no matter how bad the world may look or how rugged life may appear to be. We must take the risk of treating our children as human beings. We must take the risk of being human ourselves. We must take the risk of faith. That is what it takes for real freedom. It's what St. Paul kept telling people, as can be seen in the quote above.

Freedom has come to have a bad name in our time. Some are afraid even to use the word, because it has been so often misused. Freedom to be yourself doesn't mean very much if the lives of other people are wrecked in the process. Freedom to "do your thing" has practically no meaning when it contributes little or nothing to our common humanity and causes self-destruction. Whatever we want to call it, that is not freedom.

True freedom has some kind of worthy purpose behind it. It

can't be imposed. It has to grow out of the person. The man who sees no purpose in life, has no direction, doesn't look forward to anything will probably never be free. It takes faith to be free.

Whenever we talk about faith in this world of ours, we have to face up to God. In our secular society, we talk a lot about faith in ourselves and faith in each other. We've tried to avoid even talking about faith in God. The result is that, along with freedom, faith has come to have a bad name.

Secular faiths on which we have tried to build our world have failed. They don't work. They look weak, and they are weak. Faith without God is not quite human. Struggling to get along without God is not the road to human freedom. Quite the contrary, it is truly human to believe in God. Believing in Him is more than just knowing He exists. Everyone would admit that without argument.

There are some who say they would like to believe in God, but they don't see how they can. They've almost convinced themselves because the facts, they say, are against God. Everything in the world is perfectly ordinary; there is nothing extraordinary about life. Life is a humdrum thing, there's nothing you can do about that. Death is inevitable, and that's the end. People don't know it for sure, but it's the kind of faith they have. This is the way things are, and that is how they will be. Such faith, as we have found out, does not contribute to human freedom. It is a kind of bondage which people accept because they think there is no way out. It's like a sentence to prison of your own making, when you say you would like to believe in God, but you can't.

I believe in God and, in a way, I could say that I know Him in Jesus. It's the way St. Paul knew Him. He often said, after coming face to face with Jesus, "The God who said, 'Out of darkness the light shall shine!' is the same God who made his light shine in our hearts, to bring us the light of the knowledge of God's glory, shining in the face of Christ" (2 Cor. 4:6 TEV).

God was and is in Jesus. I believe as St. Paul did, that God was and is in Jesus reconciling the world to himself, not counting our sins against us. The Bible tells us that Jesus is the Word of God. I believe that.

Jesus died for our sins. He could do that because He was the Son of God. He died, not for himself, but for us. We don't like to hear about God, because of our failure to live up to our responsibilities as human beings. But that didn't stop God, He went ahead anyway. In Jesus, God was reconciling the whole world to himself, taking into His own heart what is wrong in us and putting us right with Him. It's about the biggest tribute ever paid to our humanity. Jesus died for us. I believe that.

God raised Jesus from the dead, giving Him a name that is above every name, that at the name of Jesus every knee should bow, of things in heaven, and things on earth, and things under the earth, that every tongue might confess that Jesus Christ is Lord. When He had by himself purged our sins, He was set down at the right hand of the majesty on high. That's Jesus Christ. *He lives*. He is Lord.

Knowing Jesus, we can know God too. We can say "I know God," as far as it is possible for a human to know Him. I know that God loves and God cares. Knowing that gives me a new grip on life every morning. Every day is a new day. Love of God, as I see it in Jesus, makes everything new. I believe in God, have confidence in Him, and trust Him to do what is right and good. I have faith that every day is a new beginning and I am free to live it. We can all know that and be free that same way in Jesus.

It takes faith, faith in God, to be truly free. St. Paul challenges us to have faith and take the risk of freedom. It's a big risk. What we do by faith is to bet our whole lives on Him. At times we may wonder, especially when things don't turn out as we might like. The world is turned around and looks as if it is out of our control. At times it may appear that we might have been better advised to bank on ourselves than to have faith in God. Faith is a risk in the very nature of things. If we knew what was going to happen in the future it wouldn't be necessary to have faith. If we were absolutely positive that death is the end and no one is going to be held accountable for what he has done, whether good or bad, we wouldn't have to have faith in God. If we knew everything, we would not exactly be human either. If we had all the answers, we'd probably be wrong. To have faith in God is to be right with Him as a human being, and also right with the world, truly human, taking the risk of freedom that comes only by faith in God.

Becoming a father or mother in this world of ours means taking a risk. It takes faith to make a marriage, and a lot of faith to have children. Many things could go wrong. Many things do go wrong. I've heard all kinds of excuses from people who were perfectly able to have and to raise children but were unwilling to take the risk of failure. They probably thought of themselves as free, but actually they weren't free at all. They were just afraid.

Allow me to clarify that I'm not imposing any ideas of my own on how many children a married couple should have. They have their own intelligence and should use it. I am talking about the fear which paralyzes people and prevents them from using their intelligence. Nor am I talking about people who would very much like to have children but have been unable to do so. I've seen people like that adopt children who needed a good home. Things can go wrong there too. I takes a lot of faith to adopt a child. There is a risk, no matter how carefully the adoption proceedings have been arranged. I admire parents in this troubled world of ours, who, with all the intelligence at their command, with all the heart God has given them, take the risk of freedom not thoughtlessly, but with the fine careless abandon of faith in God.

Being a parent is not easy; it can be exhausting and tear a person up, if he hasn't the balanced outlook on life which is characteristic of genuine freedom, freedom to think and act as a genuine human being with a grip on the future through faith in God.

Parents are torn these days between two extremes. One is the repressive method of raising children; the other is the "anything goes" method. Neither one really works, as most parents find out sooner or later. Severity has its place but a little of it goes a long way. Overly severe parents have probably caused as much damage to children as those parents who never exercise any restraint at all, permitting their children to grow up like weeds without any control.

St. Paul has some solid advice for all of life, especially for family life which needs to be restored to its proper place in the scheme of things: "You my brothers and friends," he said, "are called to freedom through faith in God as you get to know Him through Jesus Christ; don't use your freedom as a setting-out point for doing whatever comes into your little head at the moment, for over-repressiveness or over-permissiveness, for anger that cannot be controlled and for adoration which knows no bounds." Through love we need to learn how to serve one another. "The whole law is fulfilled in one commandment: You will love your neighbors as yourself. You will do that if you know me," says God.

That is the only successful way to raise children, in love. It is the way freedom works. Love that comes from faith in God is directly related to our knowledge of Jesus.

Love has its risks, of course. Every child is different. No two are exactly alike. What works with one may not work with the other. Only love works, and there's a lot of risk in that.

It takes faith, a lot of faith in God, to be free to love. I had to learn that for myself, and so do we all. St. Paul is right. This is the way to be a family; with all the freedom of faith in God, show love to one another. It works! It is the only thing that really works. It is what we need today.

Our world is dominated by fear, particularly the fear of failure. Fear paralyzes people. Nowhere is that paralysis more evident today than in the breakdown of family life. Parents are afraid to speak up. Parenthood becomes a kind of second-rate activity where everything is safe, and nothing good ever really happens. Parents are afraid to try, because they're afraid they might fail.

Children can be held back for years by fear of failure. Recently I read a story concerning a boy named Joe about whom his parents were accustomed to say, ''If Joe would only work he'd be at the top of his class.'' Joe was scared to death that even if he did begin working, he'd come out only second, sixth, or worse. Then his parents would discover the awful truth that good old Joe was not the brightest kid in the class, not by a long shot. To be on the safe side, Joe didn't work at all. He preferred to let people go on thinking that he was brighter than the squares who fight for top place. The fact is that his parents would have been perfectly satisfied to have him anywhere at all, as long as he was working and doing his best. What Joe needed most of all was the assurance that his parents loved him and accepted him just as he was. This is what God offers to us all. He accepts us just as we are, He forgives us, and encourages us to worthwhile living. With that kind of faith, Joe could be free to be himself. With the same kind of faith in God, so can we.

There are some parents who talk about their children with utter possessiveness, as if children had no personality of their own. Parents talk as if their children belong to them, like their cars or homes. Children are human beings who belong to God first of all, and then to their parents. The first responsibility children have is to God, and afterwards to their parents. Our children really don't belong to us, they belong to God. The greatest thing we can ever do for them is to help them grow up as mature men and women, able to make their own decisions, to come to their own faith in God, and to have their own freedom to love. Children have to learn to take the risk, just as their parents do.

Parents whose trust is in God don't have to know it all. They don't have to be afraid to admit they don't have all the answers. If we have faith in God, we can wait on God's Holy Spirit to supply some of the answers. One thing we can do: we can love, we can serve, we can listen, we can help. With parents doing things like that, their children will learn very quickly. They are human too, and they get the idea: the good life comes from taking the risk of love with the freedom of faith in God.

Freedom does not eliminate the need for discipline. Freedom to live doesn't just happen. Playpens may be necessary for infants to help them learn to walk. When the time of playpens is past, something else will be necessary. The arm of love is firm.

The time comes when a boy or girl begins to pick their own clothes. They also pick their own friends. Guidance may be necessary even then. That depends on the child. The time is never past, however, when love is unnecessary. Love never goes out of style. One mother put it this way: "When I read about parent-children relationships in psychology books, I really get morbid, thinking I've done just about everything wrong. And then God's Spirit comes to remind me and renew me. My family has faith in Jesus Christ. Though our sins are real and our failures frequent, God's grace and redeeming love bring the gift of Christian faith and freedom for us. Fears and failures disappear when a family has this faith to share."

There's a risk in living like that. There are those days when we don't know how everything is going to turn out. Faith is a risk. It takes its chances on God. That risk is worth taking. I know that for sure. We must take the risk of faith, the risk of freedom, the risk of love. Without that risk, our families are doomed to failure.

PART V

JESUS AND DEATH

26

Is Everything Relative?

Let us give thanks to the God and Father of our Lord Jesus Christ! For he has blessed us, in our union with Christ, by giving us every spiritual gift in the heavenly world. Before the world was made, God had already chosen us to be his in Christ, so that we would be holy and without fault before him. Because of his love, God had already decided that through Jesus Christ he would bring us to himself as his sons—this was his pleasure and purpose. Let us praise God for his glorious grace, for the free gift he gave us in his dear Son! (Eph. 1:3-6 TEV)

"Nothing is absolute. Everything is relative." We have heard intelligent people say that. It is an old idea that began with a Greek philosopher, Heraclitus, and has been around for a long time. It reflects a lot of thinking in our modern world. There are no longer any fixed points where a man can stand and see what is going on. Our world has gone on quite a trip with the idea that there are no absolutes and everything is relative, that there is no fixed point from which a man can pass judgment on himself or on the world around him. In that kind of world, a politician can engage in any kind of immoral action as long as the facade of legality is kept up, the businessman can do any kind of damage to his associates or to his customers, as long as he doesn't get caught. A man and his wife having trouble getting along with each other can proceed to separation and divorce. Children can obey their parents if they want to, and parents can take care of their children if they feel like it. Men can take days off from work and just call it sick leave, even though the only thing wrong with them is a bad case of sense of values.

"What the hell!" has become the password of our times. What we are seeing is a kind of "hell" disease affecting an awful lot of us. Whatever popular names people give it, whether they call it "relevance," "telling it like it is," or "doing your own thing," the end of that road without God is still hell, which is quite a fixed point.

It is true, of course, when we say things are getting better, we are speaking relatively. Better than what? Yesterday? Last year? Or a hundred years ago? Even when we say things are getting worse, that is only relatively true. Worse than what?

The disease of our times is that millions of people have come to feel and to say that everything is only relatively true. There are no absolutes, they say, no fixed points, nothing permanently sure, nothing absolutely certain. Where nothing is sure, nothing is certain, nothing is really true, and there are no absolutes, chaos is the result, the kind that we see all around us today. In a world where there are no absolutes, there is no real hope, and no real joy to go with it. There is just gloom, disappointment, and despair. We see it in the lives of individual people and in the passing history of our times.

If our world needs an absolute, a fixed point, a sure thing, where is it going to find it? I know of only one. That is God. Even if everything else is only relative, there will always be God.

God is not just a name that we give to some vague force at work in the universe. A lot of people seem to think of God that way. They know there is something above and beyond them, but they don't quite know what it is. So they call it God. Someday, perhaps, when the world has grown up a little more and we have learned how to control the force that is above and beyond us, there won't be any use to think it is God. That's the intellectual myth of our secular age, constantly struggling to create God in its own image.

We are not going to try to prove the existence of God. That would be a waste of time. We all know He exists; we sense it in our deepest beings and know that we are accountable to Him. We are men and He is God. The only questions that remain are these: Who is He? What is He like? How does He feel toward us? If He is absolute, and the only absolute in this world of ours, then that's something of which we must know more.

If we want to know who God is, what He is like, and how He feels toward us, we must look to the Bible. This is God's word, His message to us. It doesn't tell us *everything* about God, but it is His word in our language. It tells us what He thinks we need to know about Him. It tells us who He is, what He is like, and how He feels toward us. That is absolute, and there is no question about it. The Bible tells us that God does have feelings toward us, that He loves, and that He is God. No one is going to run Him out of His universe, no one is going to dethrone Him, and no one is ever going to change Him. He is God, and that's the way things are. That is absolute.

This God, this absolute beginner and ender of all things, has made himself known to a world of men in His Son, Jesus. Obviously God is not as simple as some people make Him out to be. He is a complex being with His own way of doing things. No one is going to tell Him what to do, or how to do it. In His sense of justice and in His feeling of mercy, about which the Bible speaks, God sent His Son to be a man for all men. That we can understand. Still, it is *the* miracle of the centuries. God is part of our history, and no one is ever going to get rid of Him. God, the absolute, has come to our world in the person of His Son to do for us relativists what we cannot do for ourselves. He died for us to atone for our sins, He wipes away the guilt we carry around inside of us, He forgives us and, by His life, He gives us life. He is God acting for us. He is Good News for every man alive and dead.

We can pick up the New Testament and open it anywhere. The story is always the same: the Good News of God in Jesus Christ, the one certainty of the whole universe, the fixed point in our own history. It is Good News everywhere, and it is good because of God. There is nothing relative about that goodness. It is absolute. It is the fixed point from which everything else that is good has to be judged. It is so good that it made St. Paul say, "Let us give thanks to the God and Father of our Lord Jesus Christ! For he has blessed us, in our union with Christ, by giving us every spiritual gift in the heavenly world. Before the world was made, God had already chosen us to be his in Christ, so that we would be holy and without fault before him. Because of his love, God had already decided that through Jesus Christ he would bring us to himself as his sons—this was his pleasure and purpose. Let us praise God for his glorious grace, for the free gift he gave us in his dear Son!"

Now, if that is true, it is Good News to a world in which God is absolute, in spite of every attempt on the part of some to shove him aside and take His place. This Good News is God's answer to the anguish and struggles of our times. In this century, with all its progress, He is still the God and Father of our Lord Jesus Christ. He still loves and He still proposes to make us His sons and daughters through Jesus. He stills the fears of our hearts and sends us the fulness of His Spirit to empower us to live as witnesses to His Son.

It is true that things are changing in this world, but part of our trouble is that we think everything is changing. We discard the past and fear the future. We regard the present as the only reality and tomorrow as unreal. That is the kind of thing that happens to a world that has forgotten about God. Thinking we are free, we have bound ourselves hand and foot. In that kind of world, there is only one reality left and that is death.

There is a noticeable anguish in mankind. There seems to be no hope of any real answers to all the questions man has to ask. Where God once stood, there is now a great void. There is no meaning in death. That is life as our world has come to see it. No absolutes, no meanings.

As I write this page at 2:30 A.M. my mind turns to the events of the past few days. It is Wednesday morning, November 27, 1974. Tomorrow will be the feast of Thanksgiving, usually a wonderful day of family warmth and love for my family. This year it will be a day of mixed emotions, grief and joy, memories painful and precious. This past Sunday, on November 24, 1974 at 2:30 P.M., my nephew, Dominick, only thirteen years old, died in a hospital bed after fighting for life against an inoperable brain tumor for more than four years. In a few hours I will officiate at his funeral service. I was privileged to be with Dominick in his last crisis along with his father, my brother Anthony. In those long suffering hours I was an intimate participant in a struggle to keep faith in an absolute God, a God who loves and answers prayer. Of course, there were moments of weakness, moments of wavering, moments of questioning why this beautiful, innocent child had to suffer. Why this young boy who loved Jesus, whose short life was filled with adversity, but who answered that adversity with an almost unbelievable and extraordinary patience and love for his father and family and God? Why did God afflict him and then take him from those he loved and who loved him so much in return? The answers did not take long in coming. The absolute, loving and living God answered His confused and suffering children in the lessons He taught through little Dominick's departure into eternal life. Jesus loved him more than we ever could, so much so He gave His life for him. Our children are not our own, they are God's. They are given to us for only a time. What brings joy to those we love is not what we give them materially, but honest, steadfast and continuing love. Life is uncertain and short and a complete waste if we pursue our own selfish ends and pursuits. There is only one thing that makes sense in life, to keep faith with God and with one another.

Is nothing absolute? It is a human question, coming from people who want to know the answer, honestly and straightforward. In the pain and anguish of our times, in our personal and intimate tragedies, God, the absolute, discloses himself. He reveals who He is, what He is like and how He feels toward us. "This is my Son," He says, "hear Him. This is my Son, see me in Him." Anybody can understand that. That is the Good News. Jesus, His Son, is the human answer to that question. His death and resurrection is not a fairy tale humans use to avoid facing reality. Jesus living, dead, and living again, is the one indisputable fact in all of history. This is God acting, God the absolute, in Jesus, His Son, the absolute Savior of the whole world.

The God who once said "Let there be light" has shined into our hearts to give us the light of the knowledge of His power and glory in the face of Jesus. The absolute God decided through Jesus "He would bring us to himself as His Sons." This is God today. By faith in Jesus we can be His sons and daughters, members of His family, because He is God today.

God is absolute and we will save ourselves a lot of grief having that fixed point in our own view of the world. It is even greater to know and experience God in Jesus as our Savior, to recognize His smiling face upon us, to receive His forgiveness, and to get a grip on life by faith in His Son Jesus. That is really knowing God. In Jesus, God acted to change us from enemies into His own sons and daughters, to restore us to His own family. It isn't so much that we are looking for God. He is looking for us.

Whoever we are, the sense of the absolute in life really begins in God, forgiving us and having us all in Jesus. "Let us praise God for His glorious grace, the free gift He gave us in His dear Son!"

27

Where Do We Look?

My eyes are ever toward the Lord, for he will pluck my feet out of the net. Turn thou to me, and be gracious to me; for I am lonely and afflicted. Relieve the troubles of my heart, and bring me out of my distresses. Consider my affliction and my trouble, and forgive all my sins. (Ps. 25:15-18 RSV)

This is an approproriate word from the Scriptures to begin each new day. Like so many of us, the Psalmist was looking for something and, unlike too many of us, he looked to the Lord.

Where do we look? Are we looking for instant solutions to deep-seated problems? The instant solutions that have already been suggested by the worldly have brought this world of ours to the brink of despair. They simply haven't worked, and a lot of us are beginning to think that there is no solution, no hope, no future. Not only our happiness but even our sanity may very well depend on the answer to the question, "where are we looking?"

The future of the human family is in serious doubt. Too many scientists have been saying lately that they don't believe we will last until the year 2000. Their opinions are not based upon emotionalism or some bizarre apocalyptic vision, but on what most scientists regard as pure hard facts.

We see nuclear weapons piling up in various parts of the world and hatred between nations and people reaching a fever pitch. Anger, frustration, or accident could produce a conflagration beyond our imagination. Pollution of our vital resources increases each day, and each day we hear reports of contamination of our food, air and water. We are warned that population growth is out of control.

The Scriptures indicate that we were not meant to be destroyers, either of ourselves or our environment. We were intended to be partners with God. We were made by God to be creative, intelligent, and compassionate beings, bearing the image of God himself.

The occasion of an infant's birth holds hints of what could have been. His parents were meant to be co-creators with God in bringing new life into the world. Farmers were meant to be co-creators with God in sustaining life with food. Doctors and nurses, the whole medical profession, were meant to be co-creators with God in bringing healing to the world. Artists and artisans were to be co-creators with God in fashioning beauty for the world. Man was made to have God as the center of his existence, to praise Him, serve Him, to be His agent and to have his eyes ever toward Him.

We all know that this is not the way things have worked out. The one fact of life that can really be called obvious is that the eyes of most of us are on everything but the Lord. Some openly defy the Lord and boast about it as if stupidity were something to be admired. Others talk piously about the Lord but go their own way in almost every crucial decision, significant action, or thought that determines their future. Eyes toward the Lord they do not have.

Of course, we all have to admit that there are strong pressures that persuade us to turn our eyes away from the Lord, to turn us away from Him. There are so many things that attract us that are really unworthy of intelligent beings, but the problem is that most of us don't think. It is as if some blindness overtakes us, and we simply don't see straight. We still can see, but we simply don't look toward the Lord.

The world we all live in has been caught in a trap of its own making. If we don't look, we get tangled up in a net of misfortune, mistrust, and misconduct. We sin against God and against one another, without any understanding of what we are doing to ourselves in the process. We make a mess of our lives, of our world, and can't understand how it all came about. We try to walk, only to stumble. We are like people whose feet are caught in a net. We get all tangled up, try to get out of the mess, and only make things worse. The feeling of being trapped by their circumstances at home: children to take care of, a house to keep up, no way of getting away for a few hours, not enough money to get what is wanted, sometimes needed, maybe a husband unsympathetic and not understanding.

There are a lot of men who feel trapped by their jobs, caught in the squeeze where they can't advance, and where they don't dare quit. There are a lot of other people who feel trapped because of debts they incur and they just can't seem to get free of them. When they get a little ahead, the car needs a new tire, and kids have to go to the doctor, or the washing machine breaks down. They are trapped, and there is nothing they can do about it. There are so many problems that make us feel trapped—unhappy marriages, uncontrollable children, poor health, lousy jobs—things constantly hem us in.

If we're young we feel trapped by "the system"; if we're older we feel trapped by the "rat race." Some of us are discouraged because the old values seem to be disintegrating, others of us feel trapped because we see no possibility of change in circumstances and institutions that should be changed.

When our feet are caught in a net like that, where do we look? Do we look at the net which has us trapped? Do we look down at our feet to the tangled mess we got ourselves into? Do we stare down maybe into the open pit of despair? That's not the way, said the Psalmist.

There is only one direction to look. If we are overwhelmed by our troubles, afraid to face the future, then we must look toward the Lord.

The Psalmist said: "My eyes are ever toward the Lord, for he will pluck my feet out of the net." The Lord is God, He is in control and can be trusted. How can we be sure of that? Just try Him.

What's the good of turning toward the Lord? Can He really do anything for us? Does He really care about us? He does; He cares. I know it for sure from my own experience; anybody can. God sent His Son and literally sacrificed Him for my sins, for our sins. This really happened, but do we know what it means for us? Jesus gave himself for us and paid the price of His own blood. This is not just a myth, it is a fact. By the blood of Jesus, God forgives. He forgives all of us. The blood of Jesus is real, and His forgiveness is real, too. It takes a certain amount of insight to see that. It takes eyes to see it. It takes what the Bible calls faith. Faith in Jesus is the biggest thing that can ever come into our lives. Faith in Jesus understands that He died and rose again from the dead for all of us. Faith recognizes Him as Lord and trusts Him to see things through. Faith is like having eyes to see Jesus and to keep on seeing Him.

Where do we look? At our troubles, or toward the Lord? In the previous chapter I made note of the death of my brother Anthony's son, Dominick. My brother's reaction taught me an unforgettable lesson. Little Dominick, a beautiful child and a firm believer in Jesus, was the apple of his father's eye. Four years before his death, we learned that he had an inoperable brain tumor that would eventually take his life. During those four years, my brother, sister, and I, as believers in divine healing, stormed heaven with our prayers. Yet this talented and attractive child was taken from his father. His father experienced great anguish; he did not meet his loss with unflinching resignation. He was human, and he wept.

But during the wake, funeral, and burial of his son, we saw an

192

amazing strength and faith transform him into a comforter to those who had come to comfort him. My brother's eyes were ever toward the Lord. He didn't just look at what he had lost. He looked up and Jesus lifted his feet out of the net. Jesus got him walking again on high ground, higher ground than he had ever walked before. He was able to talk to other parents telling them to love their children and not take them for granted. He was able to freely give his child to Jesus. He was able to talk about his honest feelings and his faith. This was faith in Jesus, a faith that believes that Jesus is Lord and knows what He is doing. It is not easy to come by. I know, for I was with my brother and participated in his experience. It was, and is, real. "You know our troubles," my brother said to the Lord. "You know us; keep on forgiving us our weakness and our sins. We shall always keep on looking up to you."

During the wake of his son, my brother never left the side of the casket. As different people came up to view the body and pay their last respects, he would ask, "Did you know my son?" if he didn't recognize them. From the recurring and haunting questions and the answers received, by brother Oreste was inspired to write the following:

Did you know my son?
I knew him but for a moment and in that moment he taught me love.
Did you know my son?
I knew him for a short while and in that while he became my friend.
Did you know my son?
I knew him during his school years and in the past year he taught me and those around him what courage really is.
Did you know my son?
I knew him well, he was extraordinary.
Did you know my son?
We all knew him, to know him was to love him, for he gave us

his love and in that giving he shared with us his courage, and through that courage gave us a vision of Who Love really is.

Where do we look? We look right at Him. Sometimes that isn't easy, especially when we are prone to sin, but He is gracious about forgiving the sins of people who trust in Him. A mature sign of faith and trust is free and full acceptance of His forgiveness.

Let's set our sights on the Lord. Faith focuses on Jesus. He is the One to look at. His eyes are on us and He is gracious to forgive. He is there when we are lonely and afflicted. He hears the troubles of our hearts and He forgives and gives life.

In the weeks that followed the death of his precious son, my brother Anthony's heart became pressed with anguish of his loss. He knew he had to keep faith, even in the aching emptiness and loneliness of the present. He thought to write a note to his son:

My loving son Dominick,

I am truly honored that God chose you, my son, to join him in his kingdom of heaven. I pray that you are enjoying the company of my father, your grandpa, and that you will both await with joy the day that I can join you in the will of God.

Please Dominick, intercede to Jesus, to give me the strength and courage that I will need to spend the rest of my living days without you. I miss you very, very much and I try so hard to fight back the tears and the sorrow that has filled my aching heart. I love you, son, now and for all eternity.

Your everloving
Popi
Praise the Lord!

Where do we look? Where can we look except to Jesus. With our eyes ever toward Him, we find forgiveness, love, and power to live.

28

Jesus Is the Way to Die

And I, if I be lifted up from the earth, will draw all men unto me. This he said, signifying what death he should die. (John 12:32-33 KJV)

Not too long ago a popular American magazine described the death of a patient in the room of a typical hospital. The man was dying on schedule. The nurses had moved him to a private room, because it was easier to close a door on the dead then to curtain a corpse in a crowded ward. The morgue attendant had calculated him in the week's projected work load.

Everything went off on schedule. By 11:00 A.M. the next day, the patient was dead as expected. The nurse closed the corpse's eyes and called for the orderlies. The attending physician notified the relatives. Within fifteen minutes, a temporary death certificate had been signed (pending confirmation of cause of death), a release of personal belongings form had been completed, the body had been washed, plugged, trussed, wrapped in a disposable paper shroud, and labeled. The morgue attendant loaded the body onto his rolling stretcher, waited considerately for an empty elevator, and rolled it past the maintenance and laundry rooms to a morgue ice box in the basement.

At noon the next day, autopsy and legal forms completed, the corpse arrived at the funeral home where it was drained, embalmed, waxed, rouged, shaved, dressed and wheeled into the "slumber room." One day later, after a brief church service, the "duroseal" coffin was lowered by a machine into the pre-purchased grave and then was covered with dirt.

The magazine article commented, "Wherever or however death comes, Americans handle it with cool, efficient dispatch. Death in America is no longer a metaphysical mystery or a summons from the divine. Rather it is an engineering problem for death's managers—the physicians, morticians, and statisticians in charge of supervising nature's planned obsolescence. To the nation that devised the disposable diaper, the dead are only a bit more troublesome than other forms of human waste."

An English essayist, J.B. Priestly, remarked: "Mankind is frightened by the mere word 'death,' and nowhere more so than in America. At dinner parties there I have brought up the question of death just to study the stunned reactions. Most people switch off the subject as if they were changing television channels." Arnold Toynbee also remarked: "Death is un-American, an affront to every citizen's inalienable right to life, liberty, and the pursuit of happiness."

We might add that America is not the only place where death is treated as if it doesn't exist. People all over the world shy away from the subject. They don't like to talk about it, and they don't even like to think about it. It is ghastly, and it is final. It is just too much to take.

Once a year though, Christians come together in all parts of the world to remember the death of one man. The place of His death was not as quiet as a private hospital room, and no morgue attendant wheeled Him quietly away. This death took place out on a hill where the public used to watch criminals executed, and He was one of them. At least, that's the way it looked that day. "He was numbered with the transgressors" (Isa. 53:12). People got the message, and most of His friends were nowhere to be seen.

It was this man who said: "I am the resurrection and the life. Whoever believes in me . . . will never die" (John 11:25,26 TEV). He is the Man who said: "I am the way, the truth, and the life" (John 14:6). Every Good Friday, Christians commemorate His death because He deals with the crucial issue of life. "I am the Way," He said. He is the way to die.

Jesus was prepared for His death. The twelfth chapter of John records a remarkable statement of His: "When I am lifted up from the earth," He said, "I will draw all men to me" (John 12:32 TEV). It was so characteristic of Jesus to prepare for His own death. Death to Jesus was just as terrible as it is to any of us, but He prepared for it. We might say, He practiced what He preached. When the terror finally came, He sweat drops of blood, but He stood his ground. Sometimes we forget that He is the one man in all of history who could have walked away from death, untouched by it. Tough as it was, He took it, and therein lies the story.

Jesus had a healthy respect for the pain, the loneliness, the abandonment that death inflicts on a man. He was well aware, as most people today don't want to be aware, that it would come to Him. Jesus had one thing to hang onto. He prepared with conviction, and the unshakable assurance that His Father cared for Him. It was to His Father that He turned in the crucial moment: "Father if it be your will, take this cup from me." It was to His Father that He turned when pain really began: "Father, forgive them for they don't know what they are doing." It was to His Father that He went when death came: "Father, into your hands I commend my spirit." Jesus said: "I am the way," the way to die.

He is the way. Jesus doesn't just show us the way, He is the way. He went the way for every one of us, that altogether obedient Son for all of us disobedient sons and daughters of our heavenly Father. He paid the price we had to pay. The wages of sin is death. It is the last law of life. But by His death, Jesus changed even that. He upset everything. All the stuff that makes for death He nailed to His cross: all the sin, all the willfulness, all the disobedience, all the pride and prejudice and passion, all of the malice of mankind; and all the judgment that comes upon humanity because of it. For that He prepared and for all of that He died.

When death came, Jesus didn't exclaim as many do, "Oh, no, not me!" He did not rage in anger, resentment, or envy, asking, "Why me?" He did feel the pressure of it, and He was sad at the thought of separation and its sense of loss. But He accepted death, and that's the remarkable thing. He accepted all its sadness and all its loneliness. Some of His cruel tormentors said, "Come down from the cross. Save yourself." He could have, but He didn't. He accepted death.

I admit that it takes a lot of faith for ordinary people like ourselves to go that way with Him. It is faith that He offers each of us by His death. "When I am lifted up from the earth, I will draw all men to me."

Christ's birth makes for Christmas, and His teaching makes people sit up and take notice. But His dying and His body being carried off dead form the crisis point of all of history. No one can pass that fact by without reaching some decision. Either one decides to pass it off as the death of just another man, a good man to be sure, or He can be seen for what He claimed to be: the Son of God reconciling the world unto himself, not counting our sins against us.

Jesus saw himself as the Son of God, doing something He alone could do for the whole world. "When I am lifted up from the earth," He said, "I will draw all men to me." Look up at my cross, He says to us today, and be drawn. Look and have faith. Look up and be forgiven. Look and have life.

He is the way to die and to have life. It can't be said that death never laid a hand on Him. It did, and He died. Now comes the great part of the story. He died, and He was raised from the dead. Death could not keep its grip on Him. It could not hold Him. The Holy One of God does not lie in a grave somewhere in Palestine. He was raised from the dead by the glory of His Father, so that we can have faith in Him and walk by that same power with life constantly renewed, always by faith in Him. A man with faith in Jesus can walk right into the jaws of death and go the same way He went, to life. I can testify that it happens every day.

This is not make-believe; it happens quite often. Not too long ago, I visited a good friend, Father Carl Campanova, who knew he had a malignant tumor and had only months to live. I thought it might be uncomfortable and awkward to talk to him, but I was mistaken. It was an uplifting experience, a spiritually joyous experience, and I was glad I went to see him.

Father Carl knew that his end was near. Our end may also be near—nearer than we think. The only difference is that he knew it and we don't. Father Carl knew Jesus, and like Jesus he was preparing for death. It was tough, but by faith in Jesus he was preparing to take it. Father Carl practiced what he had preached all the years of his ministry.

The way Father Carl died was what Jesus was talking about when He said "I am the Way." It is possible with faith in Jesus to die at any moment without concern. An old reformation hymn says, "In the midst of earthly life death surrounds us." It may very well be that in a day of jet travel, terrorism, and multiplied armed conflicts, we can understand better than ever before what that means. We shall not all expire peacefully in our beds. Illness, pain and death are on the way for every one of us. Maybe someone reading this is experiencing it right now. Now is the time, no matter where we are, to find the way in Jesus. Now is the time to prepare to go that way.

When a man is in Jesus, walking by faith in Him, he gets a whole new outlook on life. He is a new creation, a new man. Everything begins to look different, new, fresh. Tomorrow becomes today—and what a glorious today and tomorrow they are when Jesus is in them. Life looks different and so does death. It is all part of the way, to be taken in stride.

Too many times I have assisted at the funerals of friends and relatives and I've often heard many say, "If only they had lived a little longer I could have told them or shown them how much I loved them."

Why wait until tomorrow to tell your spouses how much you love them? Why wait until tomorrow to tell your parents how much they mean to you? Why wait until tomorrow to tell your children how much joy they have brought to you? Why wait? The new life in Jesus is for today. Now is the time to take Jesus in faith. Now is the time to prepare with Him in faith. Now, not tomorrow.

The spirit of God has good news for us in Jesus. His word is now, today. Now is the day of salvation. Now is the time to have life in Jesus, for it is tomorrow's life, it is eternal.

PART VI

EPILOG—A WORD TO MINISTERS

29

Don't Give up!

Then David said to Solomon his son, "Be strong and of good courage, and do it. Fear not, be not dismayed; for the Lord God, even my God, is with you. He will not fail you or forsake you, until all the work for the service of the house of the Lord is finished. (1 Chron. 28:20 RSV)

In 1963 someone commented that "the profession of clergyman is becoming an impossible burden for anyone needing a sense of meaningful vocation. Demands for a clerical class to maintain religious institutions are now being rejected. Seminary enrollment drops year by year. Religious bodies frantically search for clergy recruits. Vacant pulpits multiply. Countless ministers seek some sense of authentic vocation through frenzied activism. . . . We are observing the death throes of professional ministry."

It is now 1977 and these same sad kind of observations are still being made. We are told that we are living in crisis as to the nature and scope of the ministry as we know it. Certainly, the church and its ministry are not altogether dead. There are signs of life and vitality and renewed ministries, for example, in the charismatic renewal. But even with all of this, the exodus from the traditional and institutional ministry continues at a disheartening pace. Not a few men in the ministry are terribly discouraged and some seem not to know where to turn. A lot of good church people are very concerned and ask, ''What's happening to the ministry? Why are so many leaving? Why do those who remain seem drained and exhausted?''

The message of this chapter is intended for my brothers and co-workers in the ministry specifically, but I invite all to share the message. There is something in it for all of us.

To my brothers in the service of the kingdom, I think I owe more than pious and polite observations about the crisis in today's ministry. I have talked to many of my fellow workers and know where they are at, because I've been there myself. Many of us are not too convinced that our lives and our vocations are of any practical value, either to ourselves or the people we try to serve. We work hard, but as the years go by neither we nor our people seem to change. The problems are still there, and they come to look more and more insuperable. I know the obstacles we face in the ministry and how they tear us up. I hope to convince anyone who is there that, although my message may sound simplistic and pious, it isn't. What I have to say is, ''Don't give up! Have courage, brother!''

I'm very grateful to the good people who have said that to me in the rocky course of my own ministy. These people got the message from the same place this message originates: the crucible of faith. Faith extracts that courage from God himself, and it does that when it is living faith in God who made everything and redeemed everyone; when it is faith in Jesus, who was willing to go down into the depths for the souls of men and came out alive from His grave with life in His hands, offering it to everyone. Faith overcomes when it's got the power of God's Holy Spirit in it, not just to talk but to act, to take a stand, and to make a move in the face of deadening apathy and chaotic unrest.

People with faith have helped me many times. When I was down and about to quit, they said to me, ''Don't give up! Courage, brother!'' They got it from Him as David did when he said to

Solomon, his son, "Be strong and of good courage, and do it. Fear not, be not dismayed; for the Lord God, even my God, is with you. He will not fail you or forsake you, until all the work for the service of the house of the Lord is finished."

This could just as well be said to any Christian who is faltering along the way. "Courage, brother! Don't be afraid and don't go to pieces. The Lord God, the God who promised and the God who acts is with you." People need to hear that from their ministers, and God's ministers need to hear and believe it too.

I know how hard most of us work. I know that there are some of us who are exhausted and drained because we do too much, while there are others of our brotherhood who get by doing the minimum. There are some of us who have a lot of time, it seems, for all kinds of recreation, golf days, days off, and extended vacations. But for the most part, a majority of us are grateful if we would have just an hour alone in peace and quiet. Most of us realize that we have to have both hands on the wheel, both feet on the ground, two eyes in our heads looking for ways to get the work done, and two ears sensitive enough to hear even the snide remarks about ministers having the softest job on earth. Strangely enough, it is usually the people with the loudest criticism of the ministry who are the first to think nothing of calling for the minister at two in the morning if they get in trouble. The secular world doesn't think too much of our vocation because the pay is lousy and the work difficult. Be that as it may, we ministers are the trouble-shooters of modern civilization. People blame us for preaching the impartiality of God, and they object to the necessity for living not only with faith in Him, but also with love for their fellow men. But when they make a mess of things by ignoring everything we say, they want us around to still the violence they have created, the hatred they have fostered, the hostility they have built into modern life.

I'm very well acquainted with what we are up against, the demands made upon us: studying and preparing to preach sermons, giving conferences, fulfilling special apostolates, counseling people who come to us for help because they haven't anywhere else to turn, helping the lost to find their way, comforting those who have had the kind of deep losses that drive some to despair, and then doing for others what they themselves are afraid to do.

One day I calculated that, in order to do what my superiors and people expected me to (prepare classes and teach superbly from 8:30 A.M. to 2:30 P.M. five days a week, be available for morning worship from 6:30 to 7:15 Monday through Friday, answer telephones and be available for counseling, be intensely involved with parish and community life, be available for and direct Saturday evening and Sunday morning services at the church), I would need two hundred hours a week. That's thirty-two more than there are in the week. That is one thing the Holy Spirit hasn't done: He hasn't added thirty-two hours to the week. What is more, the Holy Spirit has only mere men like myself and the rest of us to work with—men with our headaches and toothaches, our limited capacities, our inherited abilities, our personal and family problems, our cars that need gas and repairs like everyone else's, and our strengths beyond which we cannot drive ourselves without cracking up.

But that is not the real problem. I don't think any of us entered the ministry with expectations of a living wage and a forty-hour week with weekends off. The confusion and frustration we see in the ministry today comes more from a strong feeling among us that we are not really needed or wanted. Members of the secular community regard us as intruders, and many of our own so-called "church" people look upon us as ornaments, not exactly useful but nice to have around. More and more of us in the ministry are becoming unsure whether our whole life and work really count for something. The problem becomes further complicated and discouraging when the "system" seems to insist upon treating us like children instead of responsible, thinking and mature co-workers. Many times it is precisely at that point, when we desperately try to exercise mature responsible thinking, that we may get into trouble with the leaders of the "system." Critics of the church keep on pointing out that the church and its ministry are preoccupied with preserving themselves and as a result have lost any real sense of mission of service.

All too often this is sadly true. The church often acts like a social club, engaging in all the politics, personal jealousies, backbiting, and futility that organizations undergo in order to prove to themselves that they are alive. Most of us find ourselves trapped and paralyzed by the system and some of us begin to drift in the empty hope that somehow things will get better. There are some in our number who respond to the situation by running, enjoying the sensation of being always on the go but never stopping to ask ourselves what God expects of us, and what He expects us to do.

If our work as ministers is beginning to wear thin, then brothers, we have a word from God for us: "Be strong, don't give up, have courage."

The first time this word from God came was through an old man addressing a vast assembly of leaders of the people. In the early part of the proceedings he had remained seated to preserve his strength. When he rose to his feet the vast crowd fell respectfully silent and he began to speak. He told them about a great disappointment: it had been in his heart to build a house of rest for the Ark of God, a temple for the worship of God. He was a man of war, and a king. Now he was going to turn the whole job over to his son, Solomon, with detailed plans he had worked on for a long time for a building he was never to see. David gave this advice and benediction: "Be strong and of good courage, and do it. Fear not, be not dismayed; for the Lord God, even the God whom I have served all these years, is with you." These words were thus spoken by a strong man and they came to him from God. That is the way the word of God comes to us, through men like ourselves. This man had not always been strong, for he remembered the fear, the doubt, and the heart-sickness over one of his sons, the apple of his eye, who had turned against him. He never could forget the day that son died when he cried in anguish, "Absalom, Absalom, my son, I wish it had been I instead of you."

As a mortal man, a husband, and a father, he knew the pain of life. Still he trusted God, a God with a plan, a plan he could not personally carry out. When we trust God as David did, the whole world opens up. Sometimes the truth is disclosed only after hard experience, the kind which makes a man wonder whether he really will be able to see it through. Out of that experience, his faith made strong by trial, he could say, "Don't give up! Have courage, my son!"

Those of us in the ministry know our own deficiencies. We know how hard it is to be obedient to God, and how confused we can get with all the "sincere" voices calling us from all sides. Meeting high standards calls for strong men. Standing up in a day of confusion and strident denunciation calls for men of God, men of prayer, with light in their eyes and hope in their hearts. That light and that hope is Jesus Christ himself. His birth was not ordinary, his life was not ordinary, and his death was not ordinary. He subordinated himself to the Father, to His will and His design. In Jesus we see how God works. He takes one down into the depths, and then lifts one up—that is how He does it.

Jesus, the extraordinary Son of God, died like a criminal. It looked bad and it was bad. It was so bad that most of His friends turned away from Him. In all obedience He laid His life on the line because His Father meant more to Him than anything else in the world. Through that obedience comes forgiveness and life for every person alive. It is for everyone, including us ministers. We preach it to others and must take it for ourselves.

The Bible tells us that for His obedience, God has given Jesus a name above every other name, that at the name of Jesus every knee should bow and every tongue confess that Jesus is Lord to the glory of the Father. Jesus is the glory, not us.

Religiosity has taken over many of our churches, so much so that God could vacate them for a year and He would never be missed. The living presence of God speaking a word of judgment and grace through the prophetic charismatic gifts of the Spirit is not expected in many churches; in some it wouldn't even be tolerated. God has become a slogan. Now that can be changed by a minister with a clear vision of the full gospel, one who has experienced the power of God in his own life. Whole congregations are being changed by such ministers.

We can't shake our confident faith in God if we don't have any. This is the unique challenge of our day—to be enmeshed to the turmoil and the doubt, to feel with those who wonder where God is amid all the evil and suffering, and then through a deeply personal and real experience, be able to stand up in that seething unrest, drawing on God's own power through His word, and proclaim that word with power.

God is *alive*, brothers. *He lives*! We have to know that for ourselves first and then proclaim it to our people.

I know how some of us agonize over our theology. Research, debate, and footnotes have their place in our intellectual preparation, but nothing can take the place of the reality of Jesus' Incarnation, Atonement, Resurrection, and sending of the Holy Spirit. This is God present and acting, rescuing men, healing the broken, loving the alienated, offering life for death. In the cross of Jesus, God dealt once and for all with the problem of guilt that is in us all, and in the Resurrection of Jesus, God dealt once and for all with our hopelessness, in the sending of the Spirit, God continues to deal with our weaknesses. We don't have to share the hopelessness of the world to be a part of that world. Living and experiential faith in Jesus crucified and risen again is the antidote to our modern ills. Mere theology with all its fads and fashions fades into the background when we experience the reality of Jesus. What people are looking for from us is not so much piety or intellectuality, but the sharing of lived faith experienced in Jesus. Don't give up, brothers, have courage! The experience of Jesus and the empowering by His Holy Spirit is our for the asking.

One of Jesus' men said that He is the hope of glory. So He is. The gospel does not ask a man to minister on his own power; that proves fatal every time a man tries it. No man plays God without destroying himself. A minister is called to be a man, but a real man with courage. When things get hot, people get uptight and that situation calls for a new man, a man in Jesus, a new creation of God by His Spirit.

To us, my brothers and co-workers, who are surrounded by savage pressures within and without, comes the word of the Lord: "Don't give up! Have courage! I am with you, I love you, and your ministry I will empower with the strength of my Spirit."